AN ADVOCATE'S JOURNEY

AN ADVOCATE'S JOURNEY

MICHAEL A. COOPER

An Advocate's Journey

Book design by Claire MacMaster | barefoot art graphic design
Back cover author photograph courtesy of Gabriela Herman
for *The American Lawyer*

Printed by Printworks Global Ltd., London & Hong Kong

First Edition

ISBN 13: 978-0-9973920-1-2
ISBN 10: 0-9973920-1-0

For Jeff, Sarah, Paul, and their progeny,
For my parents, and
For my resident muse and love, Nan

CONTENTS

Part VI. Pro Bono Service 239

PREFACE

Two years ago, I began to consider writing a retrospective of my life as a lawyer. Why would I be prepared to expose myself and my career to the scrutiny of others? And why would I wish to impose my reminiscences and musings on others? After some soul-searching, I believe I have identified three quite different motivations for reducing to writing a self-portrait of my life as an advocate.

First, I want my descendants to have some notion of who I was, even if the persona is distilled in large part from an account of my professional life. That focus seems appropriate, for I have spent so much of my waking life practicing law. I want those who come after me to experience what I have so sorely missed: My father died when I was twenty-one. All I have left of him are memories, some still vivid but others fading, his newspaper obituary in the *Hudson Dispatch*, a few condolence letters written to my mother or me after his death, a small number of family photos, and one torn tissue copy of a letter he wrote to a client when I was eleven or twelve in which he mentions me briefly. As the years have passed, it has become increasingly difficult for me to recall my father in my mind's eye. I want my descendants to have a clearer image of me, at least my image as a lawyer.

Second, I want to recount the more interesting cases on which I have worked, both because they illustrate some of the significant social issues and historical events through which I have lived, and because they have involved, to my good fortune, some of the great trial lawyers of my lifetime ("great" measured by their demonstrated advocacy skills, not their reputations in the legal or national press). Not all of the cases I have chosen to discuss went to trial. But I believe all of them were interesting because of the issues presented and the individuals and entities (lawyers, judges, clients, other litigants and witnesses) who participated.

My final objective, simply stated, is to render an accounting of my decades as a lawyer. I hope this retrospective will illustrate my conviction that a lawyer's life, at its fullest, has three dimensions: first, one's primary occupation (law firm lawyer, government lawyer, academic, in-house counsel, etc.); second, service to the legal profession through bar associations and otherwise; and, finally, pro bono/public interest work. For me, a lawyer's life lacking any of these dimensions will not have been complete. I have tried to live them all.

Sullivan & Cromwell (now Sullivan & Cromwell LLP), the living organism in which I have spent more than a half-century as a lawyer, is not today the firm I joined as an associate in 1960—the year John F. Kennedy was elected President. The practice of law has undergone seismic changes during the past half-century. Some of those changes will emerge in the following account, although my primary aim is to sketch a personal journey, not to attempt a sociological study.

Undertaking to write about one's life as a lawyer has several perils. I have taken care not to intrude on the privacy of my firm or any of its past or present lawyers. Indeed, I have avoided mentioning all but a handful of them by name, and I hope and believe that all of those mentions will be seen as complimentary. Finally, I have tried, I believe successfully, to avoid disclosing any client confidences or secrets or any matters not of public record that might be embarrassing to individuals with whom I may have crossed paths or to their memories.

If there are any factual errors in the following narrative, I accept entire responsibility for them. I am grateful to my dedicated secretary, Vinnie Alleva, for her patient and continual assistance with successive revisions; to Brian Carey, Kim Council, and the other always responsive and helpful members of the Sullivan & Cromwell library staff; to Tony Collado and his colleagues in the firm's Records Department for their prompt responses to my many requests; to Lucy Redmond in the References and Technical Department for providing data I feared was irretrievable; to Maria Benevenga of the firm's Graphics Department, who reproduced the images in the book; and to the firm's Managing Clerk and my good friend, Dave Liebov, for providing information regarding some of the cases I discuss. I am also greatly indebted to Spencer Smith and his colleagues at Seapoint Books, including copyeditor Jane Crosen and designer Claire MacMaster, who have patiently and wisely guided me through the publication process.

Finally, I must record my affection for and gratitude to my late dear friend, Judith S. Kaye, Chief Judge of the State of New York and the New York Court of Appeals from 1993 to 2008, for writing a foreword to this memoir.

A last caveat and tribute are called for: Because I have chosen to write about my life as a lawyer, the reader will find relatively few references to my wife, Nan, to my three children, Jeff, Sarah, and Paul, or to Nan's children, Oliver and Emily, whose collective love and support have sustained me over the decades. I could not have done all I have done without them at my side.

Michael A. Cooper
March 2016

FOREWORD

Michael Cooper begins *An Advocate's Journey* by setting out his three objectives: to create a self-portrait for his family, to share stories of his trial practice, and to render a full accounting of his decades at the Bar. All three are amply fulfilled. My own objective in writing this foreword is to encourage you to join in the Journey. It's a fascinating account of an extraordinary life in the law, representing the very best of our profession and our justice system.

The text being legal, I can only begin with full personal disclosure, having met Michael when I joined Sullivan & Cromwell as a (woman!) litigation associate back in 1962. To our mutual regret, I am unable to locate any of my Miss-Smith-to-Mr.-Cooper memoranda. Given Michael's two-year seniority at the firm, his lifetime brilliance, and captivating personal qualities, surely they would have been a treasure. Indeed, tales of intriguing cases, clients, collaborators, and courts from the '60s onward are reminders of another day of law practice and American history, nowhere better illustrated than the World Trade Center saga. All in all, this is a splendid portrait of our justice system in actual operation.

Michael Cooper was a joy to work with, a flavor that shines through the pages, whether working with him as Miss Smith on a case, or as Chief Judge Kaye (as I became) on a public service initiative. The book offers a nice reward for those of us who never hesitated to call on him for volunteer assistance in New York State and around the world. He really enjoyed it! We now have written evidence beyond doubt that his innumerable pro bono projects, and leadership of several bar organizations, gave him enormous satisfaction.

Interwoven throughout the portrait, and an additional reward for the reader, are fun facts about the author—for example, that he still uses his father's desk, that he has a passion for deep-sea fishing, that he's a horseback rider (he once even rode a mule), that his grandparents (like my father) are from Belarus, and lots more. I am certain that readers will find several surprise matches along the way.

An Advocate's Journey climaxes with Michael Cooper's ten-year representation of Guantanamo detainee Adel El-Ouerghi, a Tunisian by birth. Adel had been imprisoned at Guantanamo for twelve-and-one-half years, ending with his relocation to Uruguay. Michael's deep-down emotional as well as professional commitment to Adel are evident—as they are to his many life causes.

Indeed, *An Advocate's Journey* is a first-rate accounting of many ways we all can make this world a better place. His gift of writing this book thus goes far beyond his personal objectives.

Judith S. Kaye
October 2015

PART I: FORMATIVE YEARS

1

CHILDHOOD, YOUTH, AND COLLEGE

My father, Otto Cooper, was a lawyer in Hudson County, New Jersey. His parents had emigrated from a small village in White Russia (now part of Belarus) at the end of the nineteenth century. The village, Lyubashev, no longer exists, and the only record reference to my family I was able to locate with the help of a genealogist was the name of my great-great-grandfather, Joseph Kupperman, in the voting register for the election of the Grand Rabbi of Minsk in the mid-nineteenth century.

My great-grandfather took the name Harris Cooper when he came to the New World. He settled in New York City before bringing his family to join him. My grandparents, Jacob and Rebecca, did not wish to live in New York City. They preferred to raise a family in what they believed would be the healthier environment of the countryside, so they moved across the Hudson River to Union City, where they had a small free-standing house with a few farm animals. (It may be difficult now to think of Union City as the countryside, but it was in 1900.) When I last drove down the street where my grandparents had lived, the house was still standing.

My father's first name is listed as "Arthur" in the 1920 census records. How did "Arthur" become "Otto"? According to family legend, when my grandmother Rebecca, who spoke English very haltingly, took my father to school the first day of the school year, she introduced him as "Attah," the closest she could come to pronouncing "Arthur." The teacher understood her to say "Otto," and that was how he came to be known and addressed.

My grandfather was a tailor with a shop on Broadway, Union City's main thoroughfare. He was by no means wealthy, and I think my father bore some of the financial burden of raising his three younger brothers: George, Sidney, and Sam. Perhaps that is why my father went to Fordham Law School directly from high school. Graduating from Fordham with an LL.B. at the age of nineteen, he was too young to be admitted to the bar, so he took a clerkship in a law firm serving court papers and answering the calendar when the court clerk called out the cases scheduled to be heard that day. The only incident from that period I can recall him recounting was the occasion when he answered a calendar call and found himself standing alongside Max Steuer, perhaps the greatest and most widely known New York City trial lawyer of his time, whose cross-examination of a principal prosecution witness in the Triangle Waist Company trial has become legendary to trial lawyers.[1]

Pop (as I knew him, though the nickname did not capture his reserve and quiet dignity) opened a solo law practice in 1924 upon his admission to the bar at the age of twenty-one. Over the years, he acquired a number of small business clients, including embroidery companies, textile mills, and a regional dairy. As the de facto general counsel of these family-owned enterprises, he handled all sorts of issues for the proprietors, ranging from litigation to real estate, labor work, and estate planning. If one of his clients died, my father would rush to comfort the grieving widow—once in the middle of the night, an occasion I still recall.

[1] Steuer represented at their criminal trial the proprietors of the Triangle Waist Company, more than one hundred of whose employees, mostly girls and women who sewed ladies' shirtwaists, perished in a catastrophic fire in 1911.

Portrait of Otto Cooper

Pop was truly "a man for all seasons" as a lawyer, an exceedingly rare if not extinct species today. He was also widely known for his generosity to the poor and downtrodden. When Pop died, the Hudson County Bar Association memorial noted that his "charity was without bound and…without notoriety or remuneration," and one of his clients sent my mother a note calling him a "God sent adviser and friend."

My father would occasionally take me from our home at 235 McElroy Avenue, a one-block-long street in the Palisade section of Fort Lee, to his office on the weekend. I could never tell whether (a) he had work that required attending to in the office before Monday; (b) he wanted to dispense alms to the occasional homeless person who always seemed to be waiting for him on the street; or (c) he wanted a respite from the confines of our 14-foot-wide rowhouse. Perhaps his actual motivation included more than one of those ingredients. Whatever the reason, his office became a second home to me, and I looked forward to our weekend excursions.

My father's secretary, Miss (or was it Mrs.?) Larsen, was a person of many talents, like my father. She ran the office, as my mother ran the household, and was sufficiently experienced and intelligent to be able to draft a simple will or lease, probably using one of the preprinted forms available for the purpose.

Pop maintained an office for nearly three decades on 60th Street in West New York, immediately north of Union City. About five years before he died, he moved his office to the *Hudson Dispatch* building on 38th Street in Union City.[2] There he shared space—a common library and one large secretarial area—with two or three other lawyers. My

---

[2] The only other person I associate with the *Hudson Dispatch* is Judith Kaye, the former Chief Judge of the State of New York and of the New York Court of Appeals. Judith worked for the paper briefly as a columnist between college and law school. More of Judith later.

mother Beatrice (called "Bea" by friends and family), knew an interior decorator who persuaded my father to buy a large desk, which I use to this day, and some lovely old prints, including classic Spy caricature portraits, two of which grace the walls of my office at Sullivan & Cromwell; two others are in my study at home in New York City.

I recall going to court with my father only once. It was the federal district court in Newark, and Judge Alfred Modarelli was presiding. Judge Modarelli was a large man (he had been a lineman on a successful Fordham football team at a time when Fordham was a football powerhouse) and a long-time friend of my father, who borrowed books from Pop's law library from time to time. I recall nothing of the case other than that Jimmy Rosen, who was later appointed to the United States Court of Appeals for the Third Circuit, represented one of the parties. At one point he turned his back to Judge Modarelli for just a moment, prompting Judge Modarelli to intone to all present in the courtroom (I am paraphrasing): "I see that there is a young man, Michael Cooper, in the courtroom who may someday become a lawyer. I hope he never turns his back to a judge on the bench, as Mr. Rosen just did." I was stunned and embarrassed at having been singled out, but never forgot the lesson.

Some years ago, I did a Lexis search to see whether my father had appeared in any reported case. Sure enough, I found an opinion—by none other than Judge Modarelli—in a patent infringement action named *Fisch v. Gould*. Pop represented the patentee and, responding to a contention by the defendant that the patent claims were invalid for lack of invention, he referred to the patent in what Judge Modarelli described as "glowing terms" that "suggest[ed] a need for more semantic discipline." Pop lost the case.

My education—and life—took a sharp turn when I was

in the sixth grade at P.S. ("public school") 4 in Palisade. In normal course, I would have attended Fort Lee High School, but my parents instead enrolled me at Horace Mann School in the Riverdale section of Bronx County. Three boys from two other families and I became the first Horace Mann students, I believe, who commuted daily from New Jersey. I strongly doubt I would have developed the same educational and cultural aspirations had I attended Fort Lee High School, which did not have a stellar reputation. I do not recall ever learning how my parents came to send me to Horace Mann. I suspect a large part if not the entirety of the answer is that they wished me to have some of the educational opportunities they had never enjoyed growing up. In any event, I attended Horace Mann from the seventh grade (the "first form') through the twelfth grade ("sixth form") and made some friendships there that continued into my adult life.

Some might say that as the only child of a father with whom I had a close, loving relationship, I was destined to enter the legal profession, and even I said that the choice of a profession was "not difficult" when I wrote my entry for *The Lamplighters*, a 1979 compendium of sketches of all the lawyers who had joined Sullivan & Cromwell since its founding a century earlier. However, looking back today, I can honestly say that I have no recollection of consciously choosing to follow in my father's footsteps and, indeed, have no recollection of discussing my career choice with him even once.

Perhaps the choice was foretold by the subject matter of a short story I wrote as a junior at Horace Mann for its literary magazine, the *Manuscript*. The focus of the story was the dilemma faced by a fledgling white lawyer in a Southern town asked to represent a black man accused of committing battery against a white man. Forced to choose between his ethical principles and the realities of life in a small North

Carolina community in the era predating the Civil Rights Act of 1964, the lawyer opts for the "safer" course and declines the representation. I wrote the story in the spring of 1952, when I had just turned (or was about to turn) sixteen. Looking back, I am mystified by my choice of subject. There were no black students at P.S. 4 or in my Horace Mann class; I had no black friends outside of school; and I cannot recall meeting a single black person in my youth.

When I entered Harvard College in the fall of 1953, I was not committed to the law and gave serious thought to becoming an historian, perhaps influenced by the great historians on the Harvard faculty, including Arthur Schlesinger, Jr., and David Owen, both of whose course lectures I found enthralling. My attraction to history and academia is reflected in my selection of a field of concentration—modern American, English, and Russian History and Literature—and of a thesis topic, the impact of the Spanish Civil War on three authors: George Orwell, Arthur Koestler, and Stephen Spender. (I consider Orwell's *Homage to Catalonia* one of the finest pieces of reporting I have ever read.)

Perhaps the tipping point in my thoughts about a career came when I read an essay by Matthew Arnold discussing what he saw as the two great strands in Western civilization: the Hebraic and the Hellenic—the activist (the Hebraic), which preferred doing the right thing, and the contemplative (the Hellenic), which preferred thinking whether it was the right thing to do. I believed, perhaps erroneously, that I could make a greater impact on people and events as a lawyer than as an academic, and that appears to have been my not yet fully conscious goal in life.

2

HARVARD LAW SCHOOL

Once I had decided to pursue the law, the choice of a law school was not easy. After four years in Cambridge, part of me yearned for a new setting. I visited Yale Law School in New Haven, but soon concluded that living and studying in the same building there, Sterling Hall, would be too claustrophobic. That, I am slightly embarrassed to admit, was the principal basis of my choice to enroll at Harvard Law School.

I had had enough of dormitory living and, therefore, shared an apartment my first year with a graduate student in the faculty of Arts and Sciences to preserve some balance in my life. We lived on Irving Street just east of the University campus. My second year, I shared an apartment on Massachusetts Avenue with a friend from Horace Mann and Harvard College, Jeff Kramer, who was attending Harvard Medical School. When Jeff entertained a woman, I had to find another place to study, but otherwise we had a very comfortable relationship, and Jeff was to remain a very close friend till his passing last year. My final year at law school, Jeff and I moved to an apartment near Central Square in Cambridge, which we shared with Alan Davis, a law school classmate who became my closest friend in the Class of 1960.

The transition from Harvard College to Harvard Law School in the fall of 1957 was more difficult than I had anticipated. I was accustomed to spending time with college roommates with whom I had also attended Horace Mann School, but they had gone off to medical school or the military. Though some members of the entering Harvard Law School class in the fall of 1957 were known to me from Harvard College, the vast majority of my 500-plus new classmates were strangers.

What a varied and interesting group the entering law school class was. Many had attended Ivy League schools, but by no means all and perhaps not even a majority. I recall answering a professor's question in a first-year class and then having my answer shot down by a student who I later learned had attended Dickinson College, of which I had never heard.

Perhaps the heterogeneity and excellence of our class were epitomized by a young man named Fletcher Yarbrough, who had been raised in Navasota, Texas, and had attended Southern Methodist University. Fletcher had a soft, slow Texas drawl, and it was tempting to think that his mind was as slow as his speech. To the contrary, at the end of the first year, Fletcher ranked in the top ten in our class academically. He went on to become a widely known and respected lawyer in a widely known and respected Dallas firm, Carrington, Coleman, rising to become Managing Partner and then Chairman of the firm. Fletcher also became both a colleague and a close friend, after I retained him in the 1970s as co-counsel to an accounting firm client, which had been sued in federal court in Dallas. We spent many days and evenings together preparing the case for trial. To my disappointment, our client's client, the principal defendant, decided to settle and instructed its accounting firm to do the same after we had selected a jury and before opening statements. I still remember approaching the bench for the first time and intoning with the other counsel "Good morning, Your Honor," to which the judge replied with equal respect in his voice: "Good morning, Mr. Yarbrough."

Several of my other classmates went on to achieve great distinction, including U.S. Supreme Court Justice Antonin Scalia; Massachusetts governor and presidential nominee

Michael Dukakis; Harvard Law School professor Phillip Heymann, who has been Deputy United States Attorney General and before that Assistant Attorney General in charge of the Criminal Division; and his Harvard Law School colleague and Walmsley University professor, Frank Michelman (a "University" professorship being the highest academic honor within Harvard University), who helped draft the post-Apartheid South Africa Constitution.

Other classmates who have achieved distinction included Richard S. Arnold, Chief Judge of the United States Court of Appeals for the Eighth Circuit[3]; Judge Albert M. Rosenblatt of the New York Court of Appeals; William Ruckelshaus, the first Administrator of the Environmental Protection Agency; Mike Armstrong, Queens County District Attorney and Chief Counsel to the "Knapp Commission," which investigated charges of corruption in the New York City Police Department; and Alan J. Davis, distinguished advocate and City Solicitor of Philadelphia.

Perhaps the epitome of the "man for all seasons" in our class was Fritz Schwarz, who not only has had a fine career in private practice as a litigation partner at Cravath, Swaine & Moore, but also served as Chief Counsel to the U.S. Senate Select Committee on Intelligence (known as the "Church Committee" after its chairman, Senator Frank Church), Corporation Counsel of the City of New York, Chair of the New York City Charter Revision Commission, President of Atlantic Philanthropies, Chair of the Natural Resources Defense Council, and Senior Counsel to the Brennan Center of Justice at New York University Law School. Fritz recently

---

[3] Richard, who was first in our class, was from Texarkana on the Arkansas side of the border with Texas. He knew President Clinton and was widely regarded as a likely U.S. Supreme Court nominee. His prospective nomination was sadly foreclosed by a mortal illness and untimely death.

published a history of secrecy within our government, *Democracy in the Dark: The Seduction of Government Secrecy*, a work of immense scholarship and profound thought. His has been truly a life fully lived.

Finally, I must make special mention of Earl Silbert, a dear friend for more than sixty years. That is not an overstatement, for Earl and I met at Putney Work Camp in Vermont in 1951 and went on to become classmates at both college and law school. Earl is one of the most self-effacing people I know, but he has left his mark on history, which most of us cannot say. Earl was the Watergate prosecutor and became U.S. Attorney for the District of Columbia. He is also a former President of the American College of Trial Lawyers.

A brief anecdote will illustrate Earl's professionalism. When I took my family to Washington, D.C., in April 1973 to introduce my children Jeff, Sarah, and Paul to their nation's capital, I invited Earl to have dinner with us. He said he had a commitment that evening but would be glad to join us for breakfast the next morning. We had a delightful breakfast at the Hay-Adams, where my family and I were staying. Our conversation ranged far and wide, but Earl skillfully avoided mentioning how he had spent the previous evening: grilling President Nixon's counsel, John Dean, into the wee hours of the morning. Earl was then and has continued to be the soul of discretion.

I could continue, for other classmates went on to become the heads of major law firms, including White & Case LLP (Jim Harbison), Shearman & Sterling LLP (Steve Volk) and Dewey, Ballantine LLP (Everett Jassy) in New York City, and Morgan, Lewis LLP (Sam Fortenbaugh) in Philadelphia. Suffice it to say that anyone even remotely familiar with the bar and bench in the twentieth century would have to acknowledge that the Harvard Law School Class of 1960 was extraordinary.

Three towering figures cast a long shadow over Harvard Law School while I was a student there, as they had done for many decades: Roscoe Pound, a seminal thinker about legal education for more than a half-century[4]; Samuel Williston, whose name is almost synonymous with the corpus of contract law and who was nearing the age of 100; and Erwin Griswold, the longtime Dean, who was omnipresent but unapproachable.

Law school education in the late '50s (and for many years thereafter) was highly formulaic. First-year students studied Contracts, Property, Civil Procedure, Torts, Criminal Law, and Agency. There were no optional courses in the first year. Grading was on a numerical scale calibrated to the tenth of a point, and the era of grade inflation had not begun. An "A" was a 75 or higher, and there were very few grades as high as 80. The class of 500-plus students was divided into three sections, and all first-year classes were taken with one's sectionmates, which necessarily meant that acquaintanceship with classmates was to a large extent similarly limited.

Almost all students wrote exams in longhand in 6- by 9-inch "blue books," as I did, though perhaps one student in

---

[4] Pound walked every day from Langdell Hall, where his office contained a legendary circular desk, to a coffee shop in Harvard Square. Pound's only concession to the worst winter weather was to wear a knit cap. In three years, I never saw him wearing an overcoat.

My only encounter with Dean Pound occurred one day when I took the very small interior elevator from the Langdell Library Reading Room to the ground floor. When I entered the elevator, there to my astonishment was Roscoe Pound. Somehow in that short elevator ride he explained to me that as he had grown older, he found it increasingly difficult to walk downstairs than to walk upstairs. It was many years before I understood the truth and the physiology of Pound's observation: going downstairs, you have to balance briefly on your trailing leg.

ten or twenty typed their exams. My handwriting was (and remains) so atrocious that one professor, Abram Chayes, called me into his office, confessed that he could not decipher my handwriting, and had me dictate my exam paper into a Dictaphone.

Harvard Law School sponsored a moot court competition, called the "Ames Competition" because the arguments were held principally in the Ames Courtroom in Hastings Hall. Students were grouped into "clubs" named after law school professors. I was in the Sacks Club, which was named after Professor Albert (known to all as "Al") Sacks, who later became Dean and whom I came to consider a friend.

I recall being told that the case I was assigned to argue during the initial first-year Ames round posed an administrative law issue concerning the Federal Trade Commission. When I stood to argue, Professor Donald Turner, sitting as the presiding judge with two law students, threw me a curveball by asking whether the case presented an Article III case or controversy, absent which the "court" would not have subject-matter jurisdiction. This was not one of the issues we had been told to address, and I froze. I recall nothing of the argument (and could not even the following day), but apparently I answered the question satisfactorily because I received an award as best oral advocate in that round of the competition.

Life at and outside law school changed seismically for me very early in the morning of February 12, 1958, during the second semester of the first year, when my flat-mate awakened me to say that my mother was on the phone. When I picked up the receiver, Mother was hysterical. All I could understand through her sobbing was that it was urgent that I come home immediately. I hastened to take the first available flight to LaGuardia Airport. I remember looking out the window at the clouds scudding by and knowing in my heart that my father had died. When I arrived home in Tenafly, New Jersey, there was a tableau of family members arrayed on the front walk awaiting me. The sight of them removed all vestiges of doubt. My father was gone. After two earlier heart attacks, the third had proved fatal.

The remainder of the spring semester passed as if in a haze. I could dull the pain of the loss of my father only by working late into the night to the point where my eyes became so fatigued that the page danced in front of them, but even immersion in study could not fill the hole in my heart.

The semester ended ironically on an almost farcical note. As I was studying for my last exam in Agency, I received a call from Professor W. Barton Leach, my Property professor and a martinet who liked to remind students that he had been a colonel in the U.S. Army. Professor Leach went straight to the point: Instead of handing in my examination booklet, I had handed in the sheet with the exam questions and thrown the booklet with my answers in the wastebasket. He then fell quiet, leaving me to wonder whether I would have to rewrite the exam or perhaps take the entire year-long course again. After a lengthy pause, he informed me that my exam booklet had been found in the garbage. Perhaps that error explains, at least in part, why I did not receive a very good grade.

I was elected to the Legal Aid Bureau at the end of my first year. The Massachusetts Supreme Judicial Court had some years earlier adopted a rule permitting law students to appear in court in pro bono matters. One representation that stands out in my memory was of a student who had subscribed to a chess journal published in some country behind the Iron Curtain. He had received a notice from the U.S. Postal Service advising him that the periodical had been impounded, but that he could obtain it by filling out and returning a form. I recall concluding that despite the clear and I believe intended chilling effect of the notification and the dubious authority of the Post Office to impound a chess journal, the student did not have a meritorious claim because he could choose to receive the periodical. I suspect that today the decision would have been much closer or even gone the other way.

Since graduating in 1960 I have maintained close ties to Harvard Law School. Why? Because despite the death of my father, which continued to cast a pall over my life, I found law school intellectually stimulating and formed close friendships that have endured over the years. And because I feel a deep indebtedness to the institution that prepared me so well for my career as a lawyer. And, finally, because I believe strongly that I should support an institution whose graduates have so much to contribute to the betterment of our country and the world. It is no coincidence that HLS alumni include President Barack Obama, the immediate past Secretary of Education Arne Duncan, Secretary of Housing and Urban Development Julian Castro, and the youngest ever U.S. Ambassador to the United Nations, Samantha Power.

I have attended every quinquennial Law School reunion, including my 55th reunion this past October. I have also been active in fund-raising in several capacities, including chairing the Harvard Law School Fund in 1986. Although I have always been and remain uncomfortable asking other people to give money even when the beneficiary is an institution as deserving as Harvard Law School, I have volunteered many times to be a Class Agent and to take on other fund-raising responsibilities for the Law School, including serving as co-chair of the Reunion Gift Committees for my 40th, 45th, 50th, and 55th reunions.

Harvard Law School has a vibrant alumni organization. It has drawn its governing council from the alumni body worldwide, including three presidents who have resided and practiced law abroad: Jacques Sales of Paris, Emmanuele Turco of Italy, and Salvo Arena of Italy and New York City. I have served as a vice-president at two different times (1989–1991 and 2004–2010).

In 2010 Neil Chayet ('63) and I began to seek ways to engage older (we prefer the euphemism "senior") alumni. We recognized the "aging" of our society due to both medical advances and the socioeconomic pressures lowering the retirement age in many sectors of society, including the practice of law. These twin factors have combined to increase significantly the number of retired alumni in their sixties and older.

Neil and I had different but complementary primary interests: Neil felt a deep concern about the increased emotional difficulties some of our colleagues confront as they transition to the next phase of the lives. While I understood and sympathized with Neil's focus, my primary interest was in tapping the enormous potential in the growing cadre of senior alumni to put their energy and legal talents to work serving others both here and abroad.

Of the then roughly 36,000 Harvard Law School alumni in 2010, 13,000—more than one-third—were sixty or older. In 2010 Neil and I sent an e-mail to members of the Class of 1978 and earlier classes informing them of our intention and including a survey to elicit their individual concerns and interests. We received more than 700 responses, which I have been told is about an average response to a survey sent to so large a group.

We formed a Senior Advisory Network and held an initial meeting in Cambridge in the spring of 2011. At a further (and better attended) meeting in October of that year, a psychiatrist whose name I cannot recall discussed the emotional challenges of retirement; Lee Ginsburg, a retired Massachusetts judge, described the volunteer lawyer program of the Boston Bar Association; and Roger Pugh, a longtime friend in New York City, spoke about the International Senior Lawyers Project, which provides volunteer legal resources to developing nations around the world.

Neil and I also challenged the local Harvard Law School Associations throughout the country to adopt and further this initiative. The Harvard Law School Association of New York City responded quickly and affirmatively by forming its own Senior Advisory Group chaired by Henry Steinglass ('67) and inspired by his classmate, Linda Blumkin. Among the steps they've taken has been encouraging senior alumni in the New York City area to meet with Harvard Law School students spending their summers in New York City. Thanks to that initiative, I had a delightful lunch with two rising second-year students at the Century Association in June 2014. I hope our paths will cross again in New York City or elsewhere.

Of the many capacities in which I have endeavored to serve Harvard Law School as an alumnus, the most satisfying has been my six-year tenure on the Visiting Committee. That committee, a uniquely Harvard institution, is appointed by the University Board of Overseers to "visit" the Law School and report both to the Dean and to the President of the University on the "state" of the school. I served on the Visiting Committee from 2008 until 2013. My tenure spanned the deanships of Elena Kagan and Martha Minow, who succeeded Elena in 2009 on the latter's appointment to the Supreme Court of the United States.

Most of the members of the Visiting Committee have been

alumni of the Law School, but there have been a few recent notable exceptions, such as Judith Areen, Dean of Georgetown University Law Center; Linda Greenhouse, who for many years covered the Supreme Court of the United States for the New York Times; and Michael Sandel, the widely known political philosopher and Professor of Government at Harvard University.

The most notable exception of all to my mind was the chairman of the Visiting Committee throughout my term of service: J. Robert S. ("Rob") Pritchard, who has been successively Professor and Dean of the Faculty of Law of the University of Toronto, then President of that University; CEO of Torstar, a leading Canadian media company; and finally Chairman of Torys LLP, a prominent Canadian law firm.

The alumni Visiting Committee members included lawyers in practice, such as my partner and close friend Rodge Cohen; academics, such as Jennifer Raab, President of Hunter College, and Kurt Schmoke, Dean of Howard University Law School; and leaders in the business world, including Ken Chenault, Chairman and CEO of American Express. Needless to say, this group was neither lacking in opinions nor hesitant to voice them.

The Visiting Committee historically met annually in Cambridge (near the end of my term, the cycle was changed to biennially) to receive reports on all aspects of the Law School and meet with faculty one-on-one, with students, and with administrators.

The agenda for my last meeting began with an early-afternoon welcome by Rob Pritchard, followed by a "State of the School" update by Dean Martha Minow (including remarks on admissions and faculty appointments); meetings with students; individual meetings with faculty members; a working dinner with faculty on theory and practice in teaching; a working breakfast the following morning to discuss faculty research; a session on physical planning and finances; a following session on students and student services; an executive session; and then consecutive meetings with Dean Minow and Harvard University President Drew Faust; concluding with a closing session—all within the space of twenty-six hours. Between the executive session and the meeting with the Dean, Rob Pritchard would sit down by himself for five to ten minutes to organize his thoughts for his forthcoming reports to the Dean and the President. His ability to digest, synthesize, and organize the diverse and intensive discussions of the preceding sessions far surpassed any comparable performance in my experience. It was almost superhuman—and I mean that literally.

The annual Visiting Committee meeting was a rare and remarkable opening into the intricate inner workings of the Law School. I left each meeting both exhilarated and exhausted. My tenure on the Visiting Committee encompassed two deanships; a drastic decline in the endowment following the financial meltdown of 2008–09; the erection and opening of the WCC Center (housing classrooms, offices, and a student communal area, which merges seamlessly into the Harkness Student Center); a dramatic increase in the number of the faculty; an increase in student racial, ethnic, and national diversity; and finally an increase in the number of women students to roughly half of each class.

I do not wish to appear simplistic or sentimental, but I genuinely believe deeply that Harvard Law School is a vitally important educational institution and nursery of future leaders of our profession, our country, and the world. I will serve the Law School in any capacity it requests for as long as I can.

PART II: JOINING THE PROFESSION

3

FINDING A JOB

I spent the summer of 1958 after my first year at Harvard Law School clerking for Carpenter, Bennett & Morrissey at Exchange Place in Jersey City. The firm occupied space in an office building that was one of the tallest on the Hudson River waterfront. It was not common for law students to work at a law firm after their first year, and I undoubtedly owed the position to a favor granted by, or at the request of, one of my father's colleagues at the bar. His death that February was undoubtedly fresh in their minds, as it was in mine. After one year of law school, there was little if anything that I could contribute to the firm's practice, so I spent most of my time in the library inserting new pages in treatises and removing outdated ones. The few partners whom I met were friendly. I recall that either that summer or the following year I had a wonderful vantage point to observe an historic event—the "tall ships" (three- and four-masted sailing vessels) emerging from the mists in the outer New York Harbor into the mouth of the Hudson River.

Early in the fall semester of my second year, I began to give thought to where I would spend the following summer. Leaving a recently widowed mother to spend the summer in Washington, D.C., or elsewhere outside the New York City area was out of the question, and I did not care to spend another summer in New Jersey. So I wrote down a list of New York City law firms at which I would seek an interview. An admirer of Adlai Stevenson, who had joined Paul, Weiss not long before, I put that firm at the top of my list. I had also heard good things about the Debevoise and Cahill firms.

One firm at which I was almost certain I did not want to work was Sullivan & Cromwell,[5] which was personified in my mind by John Foster Dulles, a seemingly straitlaced, conservative Republican. (It embarrasses me today to speak in these stereotypes, but I was infected by them at the age of twenty-two.) I nevertheless decided to seek an interview at Sullivan & Cromwell and to schedule it before I visited other firms, on the working hypothesis that it would be wise to have a "stress interview" behind me as preparation for interviews at firms in which I believed I would be more interested.

All I really knew about Sullivan & Cromwell was the result of a visit my father had paid to the firm when I was in my early teens. I don't believe I ever learned the circumstances of that visit, but I do recall that he had returned home with a handful of 8½- by 14-inch yellow notepads stiffer and more serviceable than any I had seen—the same legal pads the firm uses today. He also told me with awe in his voice that the firm had a separate cadre of stenographers who worked in the evenings. Oh, how I wish he had been alive when I visited Sullivan & Cromwell many years after he had.

As chance—and great fortune—would have it, my first Sullivan & Cromwell interview was with John F. Dooling, Jr., the head of the firm's Litigation Group. It is no exaggeration to describe that interview as a life-altering experience. To explain why requires that I pause to draw a sketch of John Dooling.

He had been born in an Irish-Catholic family in Brooklyn

---

[5] Throughout this memoir, I refer to the firm as "Sullivan & Cromwell" regardless of the year to which the reference relates. "For the record," as they say, I note that the firm was reconstituted as a limited liability partnership in 2002 and is known formally as "Sullivan & Cromwell LLP."

John Dooling flanked by Dave Henkel and John Raben (S&C archives)

and had lived in that borough (and, I believe, in the same house) his entire life. While studying law in the evening at St. John's Law School, he worked in the Sullivan & Cromwell managing clerk's office, where his duties involved principally serving and filing court papers. Having a strong curious streak, he would read the papers entrusted to him. Occasionally, he would find an incorrect citation or some other flaw, which he brought to the attention of the partner in charge of the matter. After a while his reputation for intelligence and diligence earned him a favorable reputation among the partners, and they encouraged him to transfer to Harvard Law School. He did so and graduated near the top of his class. After graduation he returned to Sullivan & Cromwell as an associate and in due course became a partner and ultimately the head of the Litigation Group, the position he held at the time of my interview.

John Dooling was a truly remarkable man. He was more widely read than anyone I have ever known and loved good conversation. My interview with him was almost mesmerizing, and when it concluded, I knew that I wanted to work for and with John Dooling at Sullivan & Cromwell.

The breadth and depth of his taste in reading was illustrated by one of my last encounters with him. He had been appointed to the federal bench in the Eastern District of New York in 1961, and he invited me to be his guest at the Second Circuit Judicial Conference, which that year was held at Whiteface Inn at Lake Placid. I offered to drive and arranged to pick up John at a corner near the federal courthouse at Cadman Plaza in Brooklyn. When I arrived, he was waiting with a book under his arm. His choice for bedtime reading: the *Iliad*.

John Dooling worked at the firm every evening, pausing only for dinner at Masoletti's Restaurant on the ground floor of 70 Pine Street. John usually had two or three martinis before and during his lengthy meal. As young lawyers came in, they would join his table; when it was full, another table would be added to it, and, if necessary, a third and fourth. John would sit at the head of the table (however long) and lead the conversation in whatever direction he chose. I cannot count the lessons I learned or the wonderful stories I heard during those dinners.

When I had completed my interview with John Dooling, I then met with a young litigation partner named Bob MacCrate and with the crusty older hiring partner, David Hawkins, who extended an offer of a summer clerkship in 1959. After visiting a few other firms, I accepted the Sullivan & Cromwell offer.

I had a very stimulating and enjoyable summer at the firm, though I was thoroughly intimidated by the three young associates with whom I shared an office. One, Ted Keane, had been President of the Harvard Law Review; and the other two, Ron Dworkin and Henry Steiner, went on to become law professors at Oxford and Harvard, respectively. I had the opportunity to do both corporate and litigation work, the latter principally with Bill Piel, with whom I found working to be both stimulating and enjoyable. At the end of the summer I was invited to return as an associate upon graduation.

Although I had pretty much concluded that I wanted to return to Sullivan & Cromwell after graduation, I thought I owed it to myself to explore other possibilities while a third-year student. I interviewed at a few other firms, none of which sparked an interest, and I considered clerkship possibilities. Unfortunately, my rank in the class, which as I recall was 34 out of 500 plus, did not make me eligible for an elite clerkship, and my brief interest in working for the U.S.

Attorney's Office was squelched by Abe Chayes, my closest friend on the faculty, who asked me with disdain whether I wanted to spend my time trying nickel-and-dime drug cases. In the end, I gratefully accepted Sullivan & Cromwell's offer after clarifying that I would join the Litigation Group. Following graduation I spent six weeks or so at Fort Dix in the U.S. Army Reserve until they determined that the asthma from which I had suffered since childhood was so severe that I should be honorably discharged. And so, on October 3, 1960, I reported for work at Sullivan & Cromwell.

4

THE FIRM I ENTERED

It should not come as a surprise that the firm and profession I joined in 1960 were vastly different than they are today. In October 1960, Sullivan & Cromwell had a single office, which for decades had been located at 48 Wall Street, the headquarters of the Bank of New York. The firm had ninety-eight lawyers in all at December 1, 1960: thirty-seven partners and sixty-one associates. Legal assistants, whom we used to call "paralegals," were virtually unknown. I say "virtually" because Bill Piel had hired a Smith College graduate, Emilie Kiekhofer, in or around 1955 to assist in a large litigation, performing tasks such as document organization and review that required intelligence and a good work ethic, but did not require a law degree. (Emilie later married John Dickey, a young partner, and the two of them have been among my closest friends ever since.)

Recruiting was limited to a handful of law schools, with Harvard, Yale, and Columbia leading the way. Stanford, the law school of my incoming colleague Kendyl Monroe, was an outlier. Even NYU, one of the principal law schools from which the firm draws its lawyers today, had only one graduate, an associate, in the ranks of Sullivan & Cromwell lawyers in 1960.

When I began at the firm, I was one of fourteen Class of 1960 law school graduates to enter the office. Twelve of us began work that year, and two the following year. I have not the slightest doubt that we were the largest cadre of entering associates in the firm's history. The firm did not have office space for all of us, so I had one of six desks that had been placed around the perimeter of a conference room. Normally, however, associates started in three- or four-person offices. An associate did not have his own office till his fifth or sixth year. Associates did not have secretaries, not even shared secretaries. Any "typing" work was performed by the secretarial pool, which in my case was located on a different floor.

There was a strict dress code. You wore a suit on weekdays and even on Saturday, unless you were leaving early Saturday to attend an Ivy League football game, in which case a sport jacket and tie were acceptable. It is laughable looking back, but one day a litigation partner named Roy Steyer offered the friendly suggestion to me that I purchase a fedora because wearing one would make me appear more "professional." I drew the line at that point (largely because I thought I looked foolish in a fedora). Roy, as it turned out, not only was a gifted lawyer, but became a close friend. Although the relationships between partners and associates were superficially formal, it was nevertheless possible to form a true friendship with someone twenty-five or thirty-five years older, as I did with Roy and other litigation partners, including Marvin Schwartz, Bill Willis, Judge Peck, and Bill Piel.

It was normal to work in the office late into the night. Louis Auchincloss, a Sullivan & Cromwell associate who went on to become a celebrated novelist, was once asked whether he was required to work nights at the office. He is reported to have paused before responding: "I don't know." Saturday was generally viewed as a workday, and I and other young lawyers were also frequently in the office Sundays as well. Vacations for associates (at least for this associate) were brief and infrequent. Associates who were deemed worthy of admission to the partnership were normally invited to join after eight years.

I was surprised to learn that Sullivan & Cromwell had had a woman associate as far back as the 1930s. During my summer at the firm in 1959, I shared an office with a woman associate in the Litigation Group. When I arrived in October 1960, there were two women "permanent" associates in the Trusts & Estates Group. There were no women partners.

In 1962 Judith Smith, a graduate of NYU Law School, joined our Litigation Group. You will recognize her as former Chief Judge Judith Kaye of New York State and of the New York Court of Appeals. She married Steve Kaye, a former senior Litigation Group associate, after she and he had left the firm. I have attended many events at which Judith has spoken, and when she has spied me in the audience, she has often recalled her too brief tenure at Sullivan & Cromwell, which according to her was the only law firm that offered her a job. She has also asserted with conviction that she still has somewhere in her vast archives a memorandum (which she can no longer find) authored by her and addressed to "Mr. Cooper."

Ever since I arrived at S&C in 1960, the firm has had a small number of foreign lawyers who have come to serve as interns for a year or two before returning home. There are scores of these Sullivan & Cromwell "alumni" in many countries throughout the world.

Word processors were unknown in 1960. If you wished to write a letter, you did so on a keyboard typewriter. If you made a mistake on the keyboard, you had to erase the misspelled word, a process that was particularly difficult with carbon copies, which tended to smudge. I believe that I introduced the first electronic typewriter—the IBM mag card—to the office in the mid-'70s after I had seen one at a Miami law firm. The Xerox Corporation was still relatively new to the scene; copies were normally made on an Addressograph-Multigraph machine on paper that yellowed and crinkled with age.

Let me give you a striking example of how life in the Litigation Group has changed over a half-century. In the spring of 1961, Sullivan & Cromwell was retained to represent Chase Brass & Copper Co., a subsidiary of Kennecott Copper Corporation, in an Antitrust Division investigation of suspected price-fixing in the markets for copper and brass pipe, tube, rod, wire, sheet, and strip. Bill Piel was the partner in charge, and I the sole associate assisting him at the outset. I culled two to three thousand documents from Chase's files to respond to an Antitrust Division grand jury subpoena. I personally created index cards for every single document produced by Chase, using a numerical code I concocted like the old duodecimal system employed by libraries, so that I could, by thumbing through the index cards, identify every document constituting, referring to, or reflecting a communication between a particular Chase official and a competitor regarding the pricing of, for example, brass sheet. Today, those files would have been scanned and a document of the sort I have just described could be found instantaneously by a computer word search.

The firm's corporate and litigation clients were almost exclusively large business enterprises, including the Standard Oil Company of New Jersey (since renamed Exxon, and now ExxonMobil). Kennecott Copper Corporation, American Metal Climax (renamed AMAX), The International Nickel Company of Canada (Inco), and investment banking firms, most notably Goldman Sachs & Co., First Boston Corp., and Bache. (Of those seven organizations, only ExxonMobil and Goldman Sachs still exist as separate entities.)

Client relationships were longstanding and close; the senior corporate partner at Sullivan & Cromwell was a trusted adviser to the client on matters of import, and his judgment was occasionally sought on issues that were not strictly legal. There was no need at Sullivan & Cromwell for "client" or "business" "development." Indeed, those terms were unknown.

5

FOUR BRIEF SKETCHES

A law firm is, after all, no more than a collection of individuals: partners, retired partners retained as Of Counsel, special counsel, associates, and supporting non-lawyer staff. So a description of Sullivan & Cromwell when I entered the firm more than a half-century ago would be an empty canvas without a portrait of at least a few of the firm's lawyers. I will sketch four of them, as I have already sketched John Dooling.

Arthur H. Dean

Arthur H. Dean was the head of the firm when I started. He had succeeded John Foster Dulles in that position in 1949 and continued till 1972, a tenure that has not since been and almost certainly never will be equaled. Mr. Dean—I find it uncomfortable to refer to him otherwise—had been raised in Ithaca, New York, received both his undergraduate and law degrees from Cornell University, and maintained a close relationship with that university throughout his life, serving as Chairman of the Board from 1958 to 1968. In addition to a distinguished career as both a corporate lawyer and a litigator (he was lead counsel for the seventeen defendants in the fabled investment bankers antitrust case), he had a remarkable and varied career in public service, including service as U.S. Representative at the Panmunjom negotiations that bought an end to the Korean War and Chief of Delegation at the eighty-eight-nation conferences on the Law of the Sea in 1958 and 1960.

To an incoming associate, Mr. Dean was not approachable as the senior partner of the firm, but he was clearly conscious of his leadership position. At Christmastime for

Arthur H. Dean with Pres. Kennedy, Vice-Pres. Johnson and Sec'y of State Rusk (UPI)

a number of years, he had a roast turkey delivered to every associate's home (and for all I know every partner's), and he hosted all lawyers at his home in Oyster Bay after the firm's annual summer outing at the Piping Rock Club.

Mr. Dean had a strong sense of decency and loyalty to the firm as an entity and to all of its lawyers as individuals. I was the beneficiary of those qualities on two occasions. The first involved a dispute among the owners of the fee, the ground lease, and the operating lease of the St. Regis Hotel property on Fifth Avenue in Manhattan. Sullivan & Cromwell represented European-American Bank, which either owned or had a security interest in the ground lease. One day I had a difficult conversation with Milton Pollack, a lawyer who represented one of the other parties (and who later became a federal judge). The conversation ended with Pollack suggesting bluntly to me, a whipper-snapper, that I confer with Arthur Dean, who (he implied) would tell me the error of my view. I had never met with Mr. Dean and with some trepidation sought an audience with him. (I use the word "audience" advisedly. A young lawyer did not simply drop in for a chat with Mr. Dean.) He listened to my description of the issues and my differences with Milton Pollack, and he unhesitatingly backed me up. I had considerable pleasure in passing on his corroboration to Milton Pollack.

The other occasion was of greater import to me personally. One day, when I was a senior associate or young partner, Mr. Dean called me to his office and asked me to take charge of a new public service matter for the Town of Oyster Bay, of which he was or had been Mayor. The Town had been sued by a group of minority town workers who objected to a municipal requirement that all workers of that category reside within the town. The plaintiffs claimed that they and other minority workers could not afford to live in

Oyster Bay and that the residence requirement violated their civil rights.

I went home that evening with a heavy heart. The merits aside, I felt deeply uncomfortable about opposing civil rights claimants. (I hasten to add that this incident occurred many years before I became active in the Lawyers' Committee for Civil Rights Under Law.) I did not sleep at all that night and rose around 5 a.m. to come to the office, where I wrote a note telling Mr. Dean of my discomfort and my conviction that the Town would not be well served by having me as its advocate. I recall telling Mr. Dean that I could not professionally justify my position, and I closed with an aphorism by Montesqieu: "*Le coeur a ses raisons que le raison ne connaît point*," which can be translated: "The heart has its reasons which reason cannot comprehend." Whatever his feelings about my declination, Mr. Dean never again spoke to me about the matter, though he would have been justified in reminding me that our clients sought our professional skills, not our moral approbation.

David W. Peck

David W. Peck was the senior litigation partner when I joined the firm. Like Arthur Dean, he was from a fairly small town, in his case Crawfordsville, Indiana. He had graduated from Wabash College in Crawfordsville before attending Harvard Law School. After three years as an Assistant United States Attorney under the legendary Emory Buckner and a two-year interlude at the International Telephone and Telegraph Company, David Peck was asked by Sullivan & Cromwell to build a litigation department, which he proceeded to do by hiring bright young lawyers like John Dooling, Bill Piel, and Roy Steyer.

Having befriended Governor Thomas E. Dewey when

David W. Peck (S&C archives)

they were both in the U.S. Attorney's office, David Peck was appointed in 1943 to a vacancy on the New York Supreme Court and shortly thereafter elected to a full fourteen-year term on the Court. Two years later, he was assigned to the Appellate Division, and in 1947 he was appointed Presiding Justice at the age of forty-three. He returned to Sullivan & Cromwell on January 1, 1958, after his judicial term of office expired, and he remained a partner until taking retirement in 1980. In addition to having a distinguished career as an advocate, Judge Peck was active in the New York State Bar Association, of which he became President in 1962.

Judge Peck was as formidable as Arthur Dean but very different. Whereas Dean seemed to care nothing about his dress (I recall seeing him at his mammoth desk with a hole in the sole of his shoe and his stomach showing through his shirt where a button had come loose), Peck dressed formally. I believe he is the only lawyer I have ever known who wore starched, detachable collars. I don't think I ever saw him in the office in any garb other than a three-piece suit. He was formal in manner as well, referring to me as "Mr. Cooper" when speaking in my presence to others, even his partners. Although I worked closely with him for many years, it was not until a few years after I became a partner that I could bring myself to address him by his first name.

And yet, for all his formality, Judge Peck could be generous and considerate. At Christmastime he gave all the lawyers in the Litigation Group a bottle of wine—and very good wine it was, one year Chateau Ausone, a premier grand cru from Bordeaux. And when we were working together during the trial of the Hudson & Manhattan condemnation case discussed below, he invited my wife Ann and our five-month-old son, Jeff, to join me on a working weekend at his country home in Pawling.

Judge Peck was the finest legal writer with whom I have ever worked. His prose was compelling: there was no unnecessary verbiage, and he made every word count. He could spin a narrative in prose that enhanced the story. In 1955 he wrote *The Greer Case* about a will contest that had come to the Appellate Division from the Surrogate's Court. Mabel Seymour Greer, who left a large estate, had told her maid, chauffeur, and a few friends, but concealed from her husband the fact, that she had given birth to a son out of wedlock. The father (she claimed) was a prominent Boston physician, who later adopted the boy. True, the facts themselves were dramatic, but Judge Peck managed to weave them into a spellbinding tale. Judge Peck also wrote *Decision at Law*, a compilation of short essays about famous cases in New York law. One did not have to be a lawyer to understand Judge Peck's description of the processes by which the law evolves case by case.

When it came to brief-writing, Judge Peck firmly believed that the first few paragraphs were the most important. He eschewed the formalisms with which most lawyers begin a brief in favor of a condensed statement of his essential points. I tried to emulate his approach in the Hudson & Manhattan case, but repeatedly failed. My drafts were returned time and again with the first few paragraphs lined out and replaced by completely different text. And then one day, after Judge Peck had taken my draft of a reply brief in the Appellate Division with him to the country to edit, I received a call from him; he wanted me to know that he thought highly of my introductory paragraphs. I have never been so stunned by words of praise.

William Piel, Jr.

Known to everyone as "Bill," William Piel, Jr. was the grandson of the founder of Piel's brewery. Bill had attended Princeton as an undergraduate, where he was both a wrestler and Chairman of the *Nassau Literary Magazine*. At Harvard Law School, he became President of the Harvard Legal Aid Bureau and was elected class marshal. Bill, as you can see from the foregoing, was a natural leader.

He was a handsome man with a ramrod-straight back. He stood out wherever he went, from the courtroom to the dance floor. (I have always loved to dance, but could not hope to compete with the elegance and grace of Bill and his wife, Eleanor.) He was a lawyer with whom young associates wanted to go to war, and he prepared them for battle by taking them to the Downtown Athletic Club, where they went from a dry sauna to a plunge in a chillingly cold pool.

I had never before been to a sauna. I vividly recall Bill peering through the glass window at the thermometer, which registered 178 degrees. Bill was annoyed that the temperature was not hotter, but he entered anyway. Every fiber in me resisted entering a room where I feared my eyeballs would melt, but I did not have the fortitude to turn away. I somehow survived the experience.

Like others of his generation, Bill had been swept into World War II and spent two years in the "bottom bowels" of the Pentagon (as he described it). I believe that Bill had at one point served in the U.S. Army Cavalry. Whether or not my understanding is correct, I know he loved horses and horseback riding, kept horses at his retirement home in Sherman, Connecticut, and rode into his eighties—a feat which I will not equal (I stopped riding last year at the age of seventy-nine, because I did not wish to reach the point at which I had to be placed on and taken off a horse). Perhaps

William Piel, Jr. (S&C archives)

our common love of horses and horseback riding contributed to our friendship.

Bill liked to say that he had spent much of his professional life "scrubbing and feeding the antitrust elephants." Among his more significant antitrust assignments were representing Phillips Petroleum in a Clayton Act §7 (anti-merger) case and Ford Motor Company in the fleet discount price-fixing cases (government criminal and civil trials and consolidated private treble-damage actions). Bill was active in the New York City Bar Association, serving as chair of the important Judiciary and Grievance Committees. Bill also chaired the Departmental Disciplinary Committee. Among the highest accolades paid to Bill Piel was his election to the boards of directors of three of his litigation clients: Phillips Petroleum Company, Campbell Soup Company, and American Re-Insurance Company.

I visited Bill at his home in Sherman, Connecticut, in the spring of 1998 not long before his death. He had alveolar lung cancer and found breathing difficult, but he showed no self-pity and kept the focus of our conversation on my recent election as President of the New York City Bar Association. As I said in a memorial to Bill I wrote for The Century Association,

> "I had traveled to Sherman with the hope of lifting his spirits. Whether or not I succeeded, he lifted mine. I will never forget the indomitability of his will, the strength of his character, and the warmth of his comradeship. Bill Piel was a giant of a man, lawyer, colleague and friend."

Eustace Seligman

Eustace Seligman may seem an odd subject for me to sketch; we never worked together, and I barely knew him, but he has always personified to me the history and traditions of Sullivan & Cromwell. He came from a distinguished German-Jewish family, which was prominent in New York City financial circles. After graduation from Columbia Law School, he joined Sullivan & Cromwell. Three years later he married Maud Jaretski, the daughter of one of the firm's early partners, Alfred Jaretski, whose son Alfred Jr. also became a partner of the firm. Mr. Seligman was a trusted adviser to, and served on the boards of, important clients of the firm, including American Motors and Allied Stores. He also served for many years as president of The Legal Aid Society, a position in which I felt honored to follow him.

Eustace Seligman was a legendary host. Each summer, he would invite the summer associates (then all young men) to his home in Greenwich, Connecticut, for tennis and conversation. He invited an equal number of attractive young women, daughters of clients and friends. He asked recently elected partners to serve as junior hosts; I was privileged to attend in that capacity one year.

He was active in, and became president of, the Foreign Policy Association and knew many UN Ambassadors. He and Maud gave legendary cocktail parties, really soirées. I remember attending one and becoming engaged in conversation with a man who turned out to be the UN Ambassador from Hungary.

I have one particularly fond memory of Eustace Seligman. In March 1971 my wife Ann and I were planning a short vacation at Rock Sound, a small resort on the Caribbean island of Eleuthera, to which Pan Am had a daily nonstop flight (undoubtedly because the airline's founder and longtime chairman, Juan Trippe, had a home on the island). I somehow learned that Eustace and Maud Seligman would be at Rock Sound at the same time, but decided not to

Eustace Seligman (S&C archives)

mention the coincidence to him because we were not exactly intimate friends.

When Ann and I arrived, we were a bit tired and lay down on our bed to rest and read. I heard an unexpected "thump" outside the front door and went to identify the cause. When I opened the door, I could see Eustace Seligman shuffling down the walk away from our villa. On the front step was a copy of the *Sunday New York Times*. We, of course, thanked him later and had a very enjoyable dinner or two with Eustace and Maud at Rock Sound.

* * *

Eustace Seligman was a decade older than Arthur Dean and David Peck. The group of partners who were a decade younger included, in addition to Bill Piel, Ward Foshay (who succeeded Arthur Dean as chairman of the firm), David Henkel, and John Raben. John was principal counsel to the accounting firm of Haskins & Sells and enlisted me in or about 1971 to take responsibility for litigation against that firm all over the country. John was crisp in both thought and speech. He liked to walk to events at Yankee Stadium from his apartment on the Upper East Side. I don't think I have ever seen an outwardly more fit lawyer in the firm. Yet, for all his exercise and determination, John was tragically struck by cancer and died in 1975 at the age of fifty-eight, leaving a huge hole in the hearts of family, friends, and colleagues.

6

INTRA-FIRM RESPONSIBILITIES

A law firm does not run automatically like a child's Lionel train. There are innumerable administrative and supervisory responsibilities, legal and non-legal. I will mention only three in which I played a role.

When I became an associate in 1960, John Dooling was, as I've mentioned, the managing partner of the Litigation Group. When John was appointed to the District Court, he was succeeded by Bill Willis, who held the position till December 31, 1977, when I was asked to assume it. The managing partner of a practice group had many responsibilities (and no deputies). Perhaps the most important were coordinating the annual evaluation of associates and making assignments of lawyers to new cases.

The former process was frequently difficult. The "can't-miss" partner candidate usually required little discussion, but other determinations were harder to reach. When an associate was lagging behind her peers, was it because of limited abilities, a personal life crisis (such as a death in family), or a less than harmonious working relationship with one or more colleagues, and if the latter, could fault be assigned? When had it become clear that an associate would not become a partner?

Assignments were a more challenging responsibility than might be thought initially. It was not simply a question of who had the time to take on a new matter. Also to be factored into the decision were (1) whether an associate had previously worked with the partner in charge of the matter (other things being equal, you wanted to assign an associate who had not previously worked with that partner); (2)

whether the assignment was "right" for an associate with that level of experience (again, other things being equal, it was preferable to give an associate an assignment that would be challenging but not overwhelming), and (3) whether an assignment would expose an associate to a new area and type of responsibility or would be more of the same.

I was also conscious of whether an associate had courtroom experience, particularly as "first chair." I recall that when Dave Tulchin was a relatively senior associate, I observed that he had had little experience on his feet in a courtroom, so I arranged for him to attend a one-week program at Hofstra put on by the National Institute for Trial Advocacy. I went there to watch him conduct the examination of a witness, which he did quite skillfully. It came as no surprise to me that Dave Tulchin became one of the firm's most capable trial lawyers and has been elected to the American College of Trial Lawyers.

I will pause here to observe that trials are relatively less frequent today for several reasons, including the perception that other forms of dispute resolution are less costly and more expeditious, which is frequently but not always the case, and also because some litigations are too threatening to a company's future to risk an adverse trial outcome. One unfortunate consequence of the diminution in the number of trials is that a litigation associate is far less likely to have a meaningful trial experience today, unless he or she takes on a pro bono case. When I was a sixth-year associate, I was principal counsel for a relatively small financial institution in a jury trial (the European-American Bank case discussed below). I cannot state for a fact but strongly suspect that the likelihood of a sixth-year associate having a comparable experience today is slim indeed.

When I was managing partner of the Litigation Group, I looked for a creative way to bring the group lawyers together in a congenial social setting. In 1981 I invited all partners and associates in the group to an outing at the Orange Lawn Tennis Club in New Jersey, where they were entertained after dinner by Jon Gailmor, a folksinger friend from Vermont.

I looked similarly for creative ways to persuade summer associates that if they came to work at Sullivan & Cromwell, their entire lives would not be spent treading pavement. To that end, I arranged trips for summer associates to the Storm King Art Center near Bear Mountain and canoe trips on the Batsto River in the uninhabited Pine Barrens of New Jersey—both no more than fifty miles from New York City, clearly suitable for a one-day excursion, and both vastly different from the canyons of Manhattan.

As conflicts and other ethical issues became more prevalent and complicated, I was asked to develop expertise in that area, for which I prepared by serving on the New York City Bar Association Professional and Judicial Ethics Committee, initially as a member and then as Chair. It strikes me as odd and regrettable that, at least at that time, law students were not exposed to professional ethics in real-world settings more deeply. Perhaps the answer lay in a perception that most questions of professional ethics are highly fact-specific and for that reason do not lend themselves to generalized classroom discussion, a perception with which I strongly disagree. I continued in the role of ethics "czar" at the firm until my age-compelled retirement approached, at which point on my recommendation Joe Neuhaus, a younger litigation partner, gradually worked his way into the role.

The other firm-wide responsibility which I gradually assumed was oversight of the pro bono work done by partners and associates. At the outset, my principal task was to find suitable pro bono opportunities, which were neither as plentiful nor as varied as they are today. To give only two examples, asylum and immigration cases were rare; indeed, I cannot recall any when I began to focus on pro bono work. As a pro bono ethic took hold in the New York City bar, opportunities to volunteer multiplied. Over time, it became clear that administration of the pro bono work done by firm lawyers was a full-time job, at which point the firm appointed Jessica Klein as special counsel and gave her that responsibility.

PART III: THE CHANGES OF THE PAST HALF-CENTURY

It is not my purpose to write a tract on the many differences between Sullivan & Cromwell as an individual law firm or the legal profession as a whole as they existed in 1960 and as they exist today fifty-six years later. But I would be remiss, and this memoir would lack context, if I did not point out some of the principal differences, bearing in mind that I view the past and present through the lens of a lawyer who ceased to be an active Sullivan & Cromwell partner at the end of 2003, more than a decade ago. The changes of the past half-century have been so numerous and so vast that I can only sketch them in what is after all a personal memoir.

7

FIRM GROWTH AND DIVERSITY

One obvious and striking difference is the growth in the size of the firm. Instead of the 98 lawyers in October 1960, 37 of whom were partners, as of June 10, 2015, there were 753 lawyers: 173 partners, 507 associates, 16 practice area associates, and 57 "special counsel." Instead of a single office in New York City, the firm today has twelve offices on four continents. Yet compared to some other firms and *vereins* (associations formed under Swiss law, similar to the DH&S International organization discussed below), Sullivan & Cromwell has grown at a snail's pace. My law school classmate and friend Earl Silbert, after serving as U.S. Attorney for the District of Columbia, formed a four-lawyer firm, which after some years was "acquired" by Piper & Marbury, the largest firm in Maryland. Piper & Marbury itself later joined forces with other U.S. and U.K. firms. The resulting organization, DLA Piper, today has more than 2,500 lawyers around the world, with more than twenty offices in the United States and five in Canada. I wonder whether Earl Silbert sometimes feels as though he has awakened in an alternative universe.

When I think of the growth of Sullivan & Cromwell, I am reminded of a visit I paid in the 1970s to a meeting of partners of DH&S International at which I had been invited to speak about litigation avoidance. At a reception during the meeting I saw two partners introduced to each other, and I remember thinking that a partnership in which all the partners have not been introduced to one another cannot be called a "partnership." That thought would appear quaint in the mega-law firm world of today.

The educational background of Sullivan & Cromwell's lawyers is extraordinarily more diverse today. In 1960 virtually all of the firm's lawyers were drawn from Harvard, Yale, and Columbia law schools, with the occasional outlier from Virginia, Penn, NYU, and Stanford. When I inquired not long ago as to the number of law schools represented in the firm today, I was told that the lawyers in the New York office alone had attended ninety-three law schools. I was so doubtful of the accuracy of that number that I asked to look at the underlying data. I was astonished to learn that the number was, indeed, ninety-three. My office neighbors may have graduated from Case Western or Osgoode Hall in North America, not to mention the many law schools on other continents whose graduates fill the ranks of Sullivan & Cromwell today. Two years ago, the firm admitted six new Litigation Group partners, three of whom came from Hofstra, Quinnipiac, and Kansas Law Schools. I doubt that any of those lawyers would have received an invitation to interview at the firm fifty-five years ago.

When I was a second-year law student, law firms did not interview on campus for summer associates. Students would write to a firm requesting an interview, which might or might not be granted. On rare occasions, a student would simply appear at a law firm reception area and request an interview, as Bill Piel had done. In 2015, the firm interviewed for summer associate positions at thirty-one different law schools (including schools participating in job fairs).

The number of women in the firm has increased exponentially since the 1960s. There are many women partners, and some hold management positions in the firm. I would not be at all surprised if a woman becomes head of the firm in the next five to ten years. From my perspective the glass ceiling has been irretrievably shattered and will not be replaced or repaired, either at Sullivan & Cromwell or throughout the legal profession.

The firm has long been characterized by its religious diversity, though that was not its reputation at Harvard Law School when I was interviewing in the fall of 1958. Jewish lawyers have historically been welcomed; the current firm chairman, Joe Shenker, is an Orthodox Jew. As a Jew myself, I have always been sensitive to religious bias, particularly since my name does not hint at my religious affiliation. I can truthfully say that I have never once heard or felt any anti-Semitic bias in my more than half-century at the firm. In like fashion, the firm has for many years employed gay and lesbian lawyers, including several partners. Gender preference is simply ignored; it is truly a non-issue.

As for race and ethnic diversity, to the best of my knowledge the firm hired its first black associate, Barrington D. Parker, Jr. ("Danny" to his friends), in 1969. He went on to become a United States District Judge in the Southern District of New York before being elevated in 2001 to the United States Court of Appeals for the Second Circuit. The firm currently has two black native-born partners and one black partner who was born in Africa. There are many lawyers in the firm, including partners, of Asian and Hispanic extraction. Indeed, the roster of partners and associates reads a bit like the membership of the United Nations General Assembly.

The firm works hard and systematically to foster an atmosphere of inclusion. In late 2014, it introduced a mandatory diversity training program for all lawyers worldwide; it has an active Diversity Committee; and there are diversity training programs for incoming regular associates and also for summer associates. The firm's diversity efforts have come a long way since my invitation many years ago to Harvard

Law School Professor David Wilkins to come to New York to discuss the subject with our lawyers.

I know that as a longtime partner I may be expected to say so, but I have always believed that a lawyer at Sullivan & Cromwell is judged solely and entirely on merit, whatever his/her race, ethnicity, or sexual orientation. That was true in 1960; it is true today. I like to think that if that had not been the fact, I would have left the firm.

The Sullivan & Cromwell office I joined seems in memory to have been at least as intimate then as it is now, if not more so, in part because the firm was smaller. Lawyers would drop into each other's office more frequently than I see them doing today. In fairness, I must note that when I moved to a new office this past spring, two young associates in the adjoining offices stopped to introduce themselves, a small gesture but one that I found welcoming. Also, I occasionally see groups of lawyers at the coffee station on our floor. The firm's cafeteria, which dates back to the '70s, is still a convenient and inviting place for lawyers to gather (though the food is incomparably better today). And the firm goes to great lengths to strengthen the human aspect of the workplace through planned social gatherings and internal publications.

Not long ago I was chatting with the aptly named Michael Wiseman, one of the firm's senior partners, and asked whether he thought Sullivan & Cromwell's office would be at 125 Broad Street when my great-great-grandson enters the legal profession. I was thinking of the rising level of the seas and the extensive damage that Sandy did to our building in October 2012, when the storm surge destroyed everything below ground level.

Having listened to my question, Michael paused thoughtfully, as he often does, and then responded that he was not certain that a law firm would need to have a physical "office" at all in the future, since lawyers will be able to communicate (as they do today) with other lawyers, clients, and third parties through the Internet and by teleconference from anyplace in the world to any other place. I must say I had never thought of the future in that way, and I found Michael's speculation troubling. Yet on reflection I believe—perhaps because the contrary belief is so disturbing—that lawyers will always feel a need for and wish to enjoy the physical presence of each other, and that the prospect of universal and exclusive distance communication can be consigned to the fictional world of George Orwell. There really is no substitute for looking someone in the eye, as I believe Michael Wiseman would agree.

8

EXPANDED AREAS OF PRACTICE AND COMPETITION FOR CLIENTS

The subject matter of the cases on which I worked as a litigation associate was quite different from today. Perhaps the staple of our litigation practice a half-century ago was antitrust law, and in that area Sherman Act Section 1 conspiracy cases and Section 2 monopolization cases were more prevalent then they are now, when the firm's antitrust practice seems to consist primarily on advising whether the Antitrust Division or Federal Trade Commission is likely to challenge a proposed acquisition or merger as violating Section 7 of the Clayton Act and, where an objection is raised, negotiating a mutually acceptable partial divestiture.

Hostile takeovers, and the corporate machinery that facilitates or resists them, were unknown in 1960. In fact, I worked on the litigation arising out of the first hostile takeover by a blue-chip company: Inco Limited's takeover of the battery manufacturer ESB Corporation in 1974. I remember sitting in a Sullivan & Cromwell conference room with, among others, Joe Flom of the then small Skadden Arps firm, discussing the strategy Inco should pursue. Flom advised that Inco should bring a preemptive lawsuit, and I spent the entire evening and night drafting a complaint. I barely had time to drive home to Short Hills to take a shower and change my clothes before returning to the office. It so happened that Chuck Baird, Inco's chairman, lived nearby, and I offered to drive him into the city. When I let slip that I had had no sleep that night, Chuck's face blanched.

The Antitrust Division sued to enjoin the takeover because, it alleged, Inco had been a potential competitor of ESB in the battery market, even though Inco neither had made nor had any plans to make batteries. With substantial assistance from our then associate and later partner Bob Katz, we resolved the suit by a tolerable consent decree.

The law has multiplied, to borrow a phrase from Judge Harold Medina, Jr., "like the leaves of the bay tree," and the areas of practice in a large law firm have similarly proliferated. When I entered Sullivan & Cromwell in 1960, there were four practice groups: "General" Practice, Litigation, Tax, and Trusts & Estates. The firm's internal website now lists nineteen practice "areas," and I can think of two others not on that list which conduct periodic lunches and circulate memoranda.

Financial services regulation in 1960 was not remotely as pervasive or aggressive as it is today. One piece of legislation, Sarbanes-Oxley (named in part after my law school classmate, Maryland Senator Paul Sarbanes), enacted in 2002 after a series of accounting and other corporate scandals, has all by itself created a cottage industry within the profession. One of Sullivan & Cromwell's now retired partners, John T. ("Jack") Bostelman, authored a treatise devoted in its entirety to the statute, the "Sarbanes-Oxley Deskbook." Largely because of the international reputation of Rodge Cohen, who took the lead in developing the firm's financial institutions practice (and also served as chairman of the firm for a decade), Sullivan & Cromwell's financial institutions practice is the envy of other firms.

Financial institutions are at the core of the firm's expanding criminal law practice, which is anchored by Sam and Karen Seymour, partners in life as in the law. They have been joined in the firm by their former U.S. Attorney's Office colleagues Steve Peikin and Nick Bourtin. Their representations seldom attract public notice; when they do, it is because they have not been able to persuade prosecutors not to file charges.

In another legal arena, after the class action came into being with the comprehensive 1966 amendments to Rule 23 of the Federal Rules of Civil Procedure, an entire segment of the bar, representing plaintiffs in mass tort, securities, and antitrust cases, was born and grew like Topsy. Two of the leaders of the plaintiffs' class action bar whom I have encountered, Harold Kohn and Max Berger, are mentioned in my discussion of cases on which I have worked.

The practice of law has also become a much more competitive undertaking. In 1960 Sullivan & Cromwell and a small number of other firms could count on a core of sizable institutional clients, who rarely changed counsel. Those clients frequently selected their general counsel and sometimes non-lawyer senior executives as well from the ranks of their respective outside law firms. Those decades-long lawyer-client relationships are less common today, and even the most successful and prestigious firms now resort to websites, "pitch books," client memoranda on breaking developments, conferences, and news interviews to attract and retain clients. The competitive environment has been encouraged (some might say "exacerbated") by the widespread phenomenon of law firm "rankings," not to mention "lawyer of the week" (or month or year) coronations.

I will not touch on the sensitive subject of billing except to say that the days of the one-line "for services rendered" bill are long gone and will not return.

9

THE EXPLOSION OF TECHNOLOGY

The "machinery" of a law firm was very different in 1960 than it is now. Computer word processors were unknown. In addition to changes in word processing, document production for a lawsuit a half-century ago was measured in the number of pages, not megabytes, gigabytes, or terabytes. So-called "contract lawyers," who sift through thousands if not millions of e-mails, were unknown in 1960 and probably unimaginable.

To me, the greatest difference between the Sullivan & Cromwell I entered and the firm today has been the explosion of data collection, Internet communications, and digitization. E-mail and texting permit instant communication and multitasking, but they also do not act as a governor of expression as the handwritten letter or memorandum did. Spontaneous and instantaneous e-mail has provided rich fodder for litigation, as I learned in the Bankers Trust litigation described below and has been demonstrated time and again. I have made it a personal rule that if I wish to send a communication that may not be welcomed by the recipient or that is nuanced, if time permits I will draft it but not send it till the following day.

E-mail and texting have also depersonalized the interaction among lawyers. In February 2015 I was sitting as one of five "judges" in the semifinal round of the national moot court competition. The mock appellate argument was held in the grand meeting hall of the New York City Bar Association. The judges sat on an elevated platform behind a raised ledge reminiscent of the Supreme Court of the United States and many federal and state courts. During the argument by one of the law student contestants, I glanced to my left and saw that the "judge" sitting next to me (who happened to an actual sitting judge in her day job) was texting or e-mailing someone. I could not believe the discourtesy of her conduct or her inability to realize (or seemingly to care) that she was not absorbing all of the argument. There are, after all, cognitive limitations to multitasking.

Text-messaging and retrieval by lawyers and the frequency and speed with which they are conducted are not peculiar to the legal profession; they can be observed in virtually every gathering and on the street. Indeed, when I walk the streets of New York City, I have to be careful not to be run over by a person walking at a hurried pace with head down and fingers skating across a small keyboard. I have long been familiar with "rest stops" on thruways; now there are "text stops" as well. All this would, I'm sure, have brought a smile to the face of George Orwell: 2016 is the new 1984.

When I joined Sullivan & Cromwell, the library was both a source of necessary information (decisions, statutes, and treatises) and a place for quiet study and reflection. Today, the library is almost desolate: when I go there to read a decision or look up some other source, there is rarely another person in the vast room. That is the bad news. The good news is that many of the library resources are available online through Lexis and Westlaw. I was heartened to learn when I attended my 55th Harvard Law School reunion recently that the school is digitizing its entire library, second in size as a law library only to the Library of Congress, so that every decision of every federal and state court, not to mention those of every territorial and Native American court, will be available without charge.

10

THE GROWTH OF PRO BONO WORK

There is one striking development in the practice of law that I find heartening: the increasing devotion of professional talents and time to pro bono work of all kinds. When I was an associate, the only pro bono opportunity available to associates in large law firms, as best I recall, was to handle a criminal appeal for a client of the Legal Aid Society. Today there is an incredibly rich array of pro bono opportunities in such diverse areas as immigration, asylum, housing, foster care, veterans affairs, elderlaw, death penalty, civil and human rights, and disaster relief. My colleague and good friend Jessica Klein oversees all of the pro bono work done by Sullivan & Cromwell lawyers. And hers is no mean task. We report "qualified" pro bono hours to the *American Lawyer*; using their definition of that term, lawyers in the firm's U.S. offices devoted 43,838 hours in 2014 to pro bono matters.

One public service matter that does not fall within the American Lawyer definition of "pro bono" is particularly meaningful to me. Two or three years ago, when my son-in-law Josh Beauregard was contemplating starting a charter school in Brooklyn, I advised him to obtain legal counsel to steer him through, among other complications, the requirements and proscriptions of the New York Education Law. That opportunity was circulated within the firm, and two partners, Richard Pollack and Marion Leydier, volunteered. Fast-forward: Unity School is now in its third year, adding a new class each year; Richard is chairman of the board of Unity, and Marion Leydier is a board member.

The growing impetus for lawyers to perform pro bono work has been strengthened by two developments: (1) the inclusion in the New York Rules of Professional Conduct of a provision that "[l]awyers are strongly encouraged to provide pro bono legal services" backed by an aspirational goal for every lawyer to provide "at least 20 hours of pro bono legal services each year to poor persons;" and (2) the adoption of a rule requiring all applicants for admission to the New York Bar to demonstrate that they have performed "50 hours of qualifying pro bono service prior to filing an application for admission…."

None of this could have been foreseen, even by the most hopeful, when I entered the profession in 1960.

PART IV: MY LITIGATION EXPERIENCES

I cannot recount all or even many of the cases on which I have worked since I started at Sullivan & Cromwell fifty-six years ago. If I tried, a reader would eventually succumb to boredom, as I would to exhaustion.

How then to identify those worth discussing? One, the Hudson & Manhattan condemnation case creating the space on which the World Trade Center was erected, marks a chapter in the history of the metropolitan New York City area; the case is worth discussing for that reason alone. Others such as the Esso Resources Canada case contributed significantly to the growth and clarity of the law, in that case clarification of the definition of "occurrence" in a casualty insurance policy. Still others were teaching experiences, such as how to conduct a thorough jury *voir dire*, which I failed to do in the Esso Resources Canada case. And every once in a while—perhaps only five times in my life—I was blessed with the opportunity to see a truly great trial lawyer in action: Judge Peck in the Hudson & Manhattan condemnation trial, Bill Piel in the fee dispute that followed the condemnation proceeding, Frank Raichle in the Cornell Aeronautical Laboratory trial, Jonathan Sumption in a high-stakes London arbitration in which I sat as a panel member, and my partner and friend, Garry Beeney, in the South Carolina Voting Rights Act case.

The majority of the cases I have chosen to discuss in some detail involved trials with direct and cross-examination of witnesses. The representation of a party in a trial is like no other legal experience. A trial lawyer's senses are heightened because he or she must make judgments, often of critical importance, on the spur of the moment, such as how to continue when a witness gives an unanticipated answer to a question. However much a trial lawyer may try to craft in advance the presentation of a claim or defense, a trial can never be completely scripted. Moreover, it is not simply what a trial lawyer says to the trial judge, the jury or a witness, but how it is said. In a real sense, the conduct of a trial is the cultivation of a relationship, and that is true whether the trial is to a judge, a jury, or an administrative tribunal.

There are some representations about which I cannot fairly report without invading the confidences and/or privacy of a client or disclosing other matters that should remain private. I have taken great care to avoid doing so in the following pages and hope I have not strayed from that stricture.

Let me start with my introduction to the world of litigation at Sullivan & Cromwell in the fall of 1960.

11

EARLY CASES

As an incoming associate, I was asked to research issues for, and occasionally write portions of, legal briefs. Two stand out in my memory.

The first case, the only one I can recall working on with John Dooling before he was appointed to the District Court, arose under the Robinson-Patman Act. Our client was the now-defunct Grand Union Corporation supermarket chain, and the issue was whether the Federal Trade Commission could invoke Section 5 of the Federal Trade Commission Act, which condemns "unfair methods of competition," to fill a void in Section 2(d) of the Robinson-Patman Act, which prohibits the giving, but not the receipt, of discriminatory promotional allowances. (In contrast, both the giving and the receipt of discriminatory *prices* are explicitly prohibited by the Robinson-Patman Act.) The FTC had entered a cease-and-desist order against Grand Union, which filed a petition for review in the United States Court of Appeals for the Second Circuit.

Bill Piel took over the case from John Dooling after John's appointment to the bench and argued the appeal in the Second Circuit. I sat by his side at the counsel table. Bill appeared to be a supremely and justifiably self-confident advocate, but, sitting next to him, I noticed the barest quaver in his voice when he argued, showing that he was in fact more nervous than he appeared.

The Court of Appeals affirmed the Federal Trade Commission order in a split (2–1) decision. Judge Clark, writing for the majority, acknowledged that the case presented "an admittedly novel application of §5," but reasoned that the omission of buyers from the statutory prohibition "was more 'inadvertent' than studious" and that "one need not resort to metaphysical subtleties to denominate [Grand Union's] conduct an unfair method of competition." Judge Moore vigorously dissented. In his view, the FTC should not be permitted "to utilize the convenient vagueness of the concept of 'unfair competition' as an independent source of power 'to supply what Congress has studiously omitted'." The language of both opinions calls to mind some of the recent U.S. Supreme Court decisions interpreting federal statutes and regulations.

* * *

The second of my memorable early cases involved Sullivan & Cromwell's longtime client Inco. The firm's relationship with Inco was unusually close. One alumnus of the firm, Harry Wingate, had been Inco's chairman for many years, and another alumnus, Bill Kennedy, was general counsel at the time of the matter I'm describing. Inco was the western world's largest nickel producer. Indeed, Inco was so dominant a player in the nickel industry that it was often called simply "the Nickel Company."

On August 8, 1961, two Federal Trade Commission investigators arrived at the entrance to Inco's New York City headquarters at 67 Wall Street. They demanded immediate "access" to all of Inco's files to determine whether the company was complying with the terms of an antitrust consent decree Inco had entered into in 1948. The FTC investigators invoked what was quaintly called the "visitation" provision of the decree. That provision entitled "duly authorized representatives of the Department of Justice" to have "access" to, inter alia, "such records and documents of Inco Ltd. as may be then located in the United States…relating to any matters contained in this judgment." Access was to be provided "on reasonable notice," which had hardly been afforded in this instance by appearing at the door to corporate headquarters and demanding unrestricted entry to Inco's files.

Bill Kennedy demurred to the investigators' demand for immediate access, asked them to return the next day, and proceeded to call a Sullivan & Cromwell senior partner named George Sharp. He enlisted his litigation partner, Inzer Wyatt, who in turn enlisted me.

The matter was submitted to the United States District Court for the Southern District of New York, which had retained jurisdiction to enter "such further orders…as may be necessary or appropriate for…carrying out…this judgment." The issue was whether the visitation clause should be treated as the equivalent of a subpoena duces tecum, in response to which the person served had the right and obligation to identify and then produce responsive documents, or whether the FTC investigators were entitled to determine in the first instance which documents were responsive. In other words, did the consent decree in effect hand over the keys to Inco's files to the FTC investigators?

I recall sitting in Inzer Wyatt's office while he reviewed the draft brief I had handed him. When he reached the end and saw that only his name appeared under the "Of Counsel" caption, he asked why I had not added my name as well. I replied that I had not yet been admitted to the Southern District. (One could be admitted to practice in federal court in the Southern District of New York only one year or more after having been admitted to practice in the New York state courts. I was not admitted in New York till October 1961 because of the state's six-month residency requirement before taking the bar exam.) Inzer Wyatt insisted that my name be included in the brief and added in a soft Southern accent: "If they object or raise a question, I will move your admission in open court." In the end, no such objection or question was raised.

Judge Metzner of the Southern District rendered his decision in March 1962. After noting that there was no precedent defining precisely what is meant by "access," Judge Metzner accepted our arguments and ruled that "[n]othing has been shown to indicate that the procedure to be followed in complying with a demand for 'access' should be different from that in the subpoena cases." After weighing the likelihood of a reversal, the government decided not to appeal.

* * *

The other significant engagement during my first year in the office was an antitrust investigation of our client Kennecott's subsidiary Chase Brass and other brass mill companies. Kennecott and most of the other major copper producers, including Anaconda and Phelps Dodge, had subsidiaries or divisions that fabricated brass tube, pipe, sheet, strip, and wire from their parents' copper. Brass, a compound of copper and zinc, is used for decorative objects because of its brightness, for musical instruments, and most widely for plumbing fixtures and electrical wiring. The brass mill industry was a tightly knit group of companies whose founders were among the wealthiest industrialists of their time. The center of the industry was located in or near Waterbury and Bridgeport, Connecticut.

I remember driving with Bill Piel to Waterbury for two days of interviews. Driving down the main street looking for Chase Brass, we passed a large complex of old, grimy brick buildings, with an "Anaconda American Brass" name sign. We then drove by a handsome stone governmental building on our right but could not find Chase Brass. Tracing back our steps, we discovered that the handsome stone building was, in fact, the headquarters of Chase Brass. There was a parapet atop the building from which members of the Chase family could see their fabricating facilities a few miles to the north, reminiscent of the "widow's walks" atop the homes of ship captains on Martha's Vineyard.

At the end of the first day of interviews, Bill Piel instructed me to dictate the substance of the interviews as recorded in my notes into a dictating machine. I had never used one before. Bill sat by my side adjusting both the distance between the Dictaphone and my mouth and the angle at which I held the Dictaphone. By the end of the evening I was a nervous wreck.

Upon rising the following morning, I started to perform my daily regimen of push-ups. Bill poked his head through the doorway connecting our rooms, and, on observing what I was doing, asked whether he could join me. I agreed, of course. Bill got down on the floor, and we started. When I reached my usual goal of twenty-five push-ups, I glanced over at Bill, who was still going strong. I continued, determined to match him push-up for push-up. When we reached thirty-five, our eyes met, and we tacitly agreed to call it a day. It was only later that I learned that Bill, who was fifty or fifty-one at the time, had been a wrestler at Princeton. No wonder he had the physique and stamina of an athlete.

The brass mill investigation spawned more than two decades of litigation, which I will discuss later.

12

MATTER OF PORT AUTHORITY TRANS-HUDSON CORP. (HUDSON & MANHATTAN CONDEMNATION)

Perhaps the most unusual case on which I have worked was the Hudson & Manhattan–PATH condemnation proceeding, which commenced in 1962 and continued till 1968. Condemnation, or "eminent domain" as it is sometimes called, refers to the power of the state to bring a judicial proceeding to transfer title to property from its private owner to a governmental entity. The New York Court of Appeals long ago ruled that the power of eminent domain is "an inherent and unlimited attribute of sovereignty." Under the United States and New York constitutions, the appropriating authority is required to pay "just compensation" to the former owner of condemned property.

* * *

I have not researched the background to the conferral on the Port Authority of New York and New Jersey (the "Port Authority") of the power to condemn the Hudson Tubes and the land and buildings above its downtown New York terminal, but I believe I can make an educated guess. Nelson Rockefeller, New York's Governor at the time, appears to have had an edifice complex. It was manifested in the enormous state office buildings he erected in Albany, which are colossi compared to the rest of Albany's skyline. He wished to erect two towers in lower Manhattan that would be visible from many miles in all directions and would symbolize the economic preeminence of New York City. They were to be named the "World Trade Center."

The site selected for the World Trade Center consisted of two city blocks between Church and West streets in lower Manhattan. The only structures on those blocks that were taller than three or four stories were two roughly twenty-story office buildings owned by Hudson & Manhattan Corporation.

Governor Rockefeller decided, perhaps for budgetary and other fiscal reasons, that the twin towers he envisioned should be developed by the Port Authority. However, because the Port Authority was a creature of compact between the States of New York and New Jersey, created to develop transportation and terminal facilities and to promote commerce in the ports of the two states, the consent of New Jersey Governor Robert Meyner was required, and the price he exacted was that the Port Authority acquire the Hudson Tubes, a rail rapid transit system that transported people within and between the two states.

The large majority of the system riders were individuals who commuted from New Jersey to work in Manhattan or other boroughs and home again at the end of the day. The transit system was in dire straits: it had not turned a profit for at least three decades; its owner, Hudson Rapid Tubes Corporation, a wholly owned subsidiary of Hudson & Manhattan Corporation, had recently emerged from bankruptcy reorganization with no realistic prospect of becoming profitable; and the transit system it operated suffered from years of deferred maintenance. Yet the Hudson Tubes remained an engineering and construction marvel, constructed at immense cost over a period of more than a decade at the turn of the century, the first trans-Hudson bridge or tunnel crossing. Apart from the river crossings, the transit system was largely underground. It maintained terminals at Church Street in lower Manhattan and at 33rd Street on the West Side, and in New Jersey at Hoboken, Jersey City, and Newark.

The deal was struck by Governors Rockefeller and Meyner: the Port Authority would acquire the site and erect the twin towers, and a newly created subsidiary, Port Authority Trans-Hudson Corporation, would acquire and rehabilitate the Hudson Tubes. The necessary enabling legislation was passed in both states, and a petition for condemnation was filed in the Supreme Court, New York County.

As far as I know, the equity in Hudson & Manhattan had been eliminated in the bankruptcy reorganization, and, therefore, the stakeholders in the condemnation who would receive the anticipated award were the original bondholders of Hudson & Manhattan or speculators who had purchased those bonds. The company's management turned to Judge Peck for representation in the condemnation proceeding. Judge Peck in turn enlisted me as his principal associate, an enormous responsibility as well as opportunity for a young lawyer who was only a second-year associate. Jack Jaqua, a corporate partner who had had some exposure to railroads in his practice, was "Of Counsel" to Judge Peck, but did not appear in court in the condemnation proceeding.

One of our first tasks was to negotiate an advance payment on account of the condemnation award. The responsibility for that negotiation fell to L. Robert Driver, Jr., Hudson & Manhattan's General Counsel; Theodore Tarlau, a solo practitioner who had some preexisting relationship with Hudson & Manhattan; and me. As fate would have it, we met with Port Authority representatives, led by its general counsel, Sidney Goldstein, in the afternoon of November 22, 1963. As I recall, there were at least a dozen people in

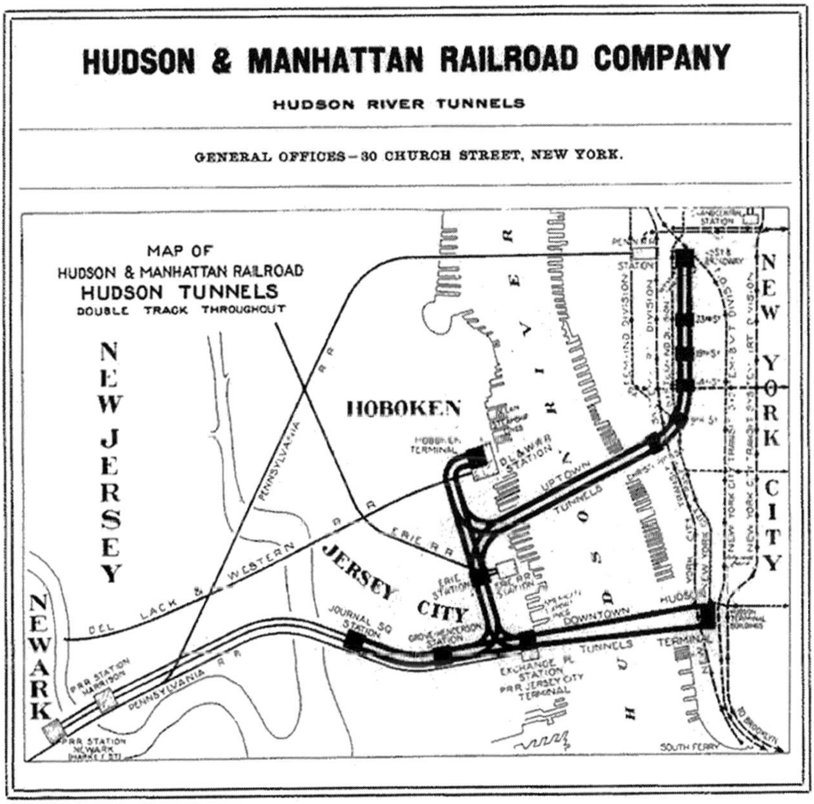

Map of Hudson Tubes Transit System

the Port Authority conference room. The negotiation went back and forth. At some point, a Port Authority employee entered the conference room and handed a message to Sidney Goldstein. He read the message to himself, paused, and then interrupted the conversation to announce that President Kennedy had been fatally shot in Dallas. The room fell silent and remained so for more than a minute till one person after another finally rose, lifted his briefcase, and departed the room. No one called the meeting to a conclusion; there was no leave-taking that I can recall; we were all in shock and simply dispersed.

The pall that descended over the country that day was leaden, and the grief all-consuming. The images of that time are indelibly etched in our collective consciousness. The best-known image is of Caroline and John Jr. standing with their widowed mother, but the one I cannot shake is of the riderless horse with upturned boots, signifying the fallen commander-in-chief.

Before I go further, I should say something about our adversaries and the trial judge. The Port Authority had extensive experience in condemnation law and proceedings, because it invoked its power of eminent domain whenever a tunnel entrance was enlarged or rerouted or a bridge extension built. The Port Authority's chief counsel in those proceedings in the early '60s was Nathaniel Fensterstock, whom I would judge to have been in his mid- to late-fifties. He was very aggressive and accustomed to prevailing over the relatively few members of the private bar who specialized in condemnation law. Fensterstock had never encountered an adversary of Judge Peck's abilities and stature, and the experience proved to be Fensterstock's undoing. His principal associate was Milton Pachter, who was as collegial as his senior was difficult.

The trial judge was Charles A. Loreto, who, I believe, regularly sat in the Bronx County Courthouse near Yankee Stadium, but had been chosen to preside over our proceeding in Manhattan. Justice Loreto was the son of immigrant parents from southern Italy. A graduate of Columbia College and Columbia Law School, he had been a Municipal Court judge for twelve years and thereafter had sat on the Supreme Court for fifteen years.

Whoever assigned Justice Loreto to our condemnation proceeding could not have made a wiser choice. He was unfailingly courteous to counsel and witnesses, and spoke softly. His mild manner masked the fact that he was at all times in control of the courtroom, even when sorely tested, as he was in this proceeding. Finally, Justice Loreto seemed to—and, as his decision shows, in fact did—grasp all aspects of the transit system's operations, economics, and demographic essentiality, and he understood the distinctive complexities of condemnation law. In short, Justice Loreto was the perfect choice to preside over this proceeding.

There were a few memorable moments in the months leading up to trial. To determine the physical condition of the two tunnels under the Hudson River and the adjoining portions in Manhattan, Jersey City, and Hoboken, the engineering experts rode through the tunnels late at night on an open flatbed car. I joined them. Assuming for some reason that it would be cold in the tunnels, I wore a flannel shirt and sweater. In fact, the tunnels were quite warm, and even after doffing whatever I could and still remain decent, I was drenched in sweat. My other memory of that night is that the underwater tunnels, which consisted of cast-iron sections bolted together, leaked visibly. Water was pumped from them continuously, a feature that I involuntarily remembered a number of times during the decade that I rode on the system while commuting to work from Short Hills, New Jersey.

The second pretrial event that stands out in my memory was our visits to the two office towers and the transit system in the company of Justice Loreto, who was required by statute to conduct a "view" of the condemned property. The visits extended over two days. The Port Authority hosted lunch one day, and we did so the second day. The Port Authority chose a private lunch club, comfortable but utterly without character. The second day, Judge Peck hosted Justice Loreto and counsel at Jimmy's, a Greek restaurant at the southern tip of Manhattan, where the patrons walked down a long table fronting the kitchen and filled with vessels from which you served yourself. Justice Loreto clearly preferred Jimmy's to the private club.

The early days of the trial, which commenced in the fall of 1964, proceeded with the presentation of painstakingly detailed evidence of the fair rental value of the two office buildings and the renovations they would have to undergo in order to obtain that level of rents. I remember being pleased but apprehensive when Judge Peck asked me to put on one of our principal witnesses.

Nathaniel Fensterstock was not having an easy time of it or making it easy for others. He continually badgered the witnesses, questioned them in excruciating (and unnecessary) detail, and was exceedingly discourteous to both Judge Peck and Justice Loreto. He did not take kindly that numerous objections to his repetitive questioning of our witnesses were sustained.

Finally, when Judge Peck objected to one of his questions, Fensterstock commented: "I understand why Judge Peck would prefer not to have it in." Judge Peck asked that the remark be stricken, eliciting the following from Justice Loreto:

> I agree with you. He has a habit of casting aspersions upon you, and from time to time the Court, and he has been reprimanded several times, and the last time with some severity, which indicated that it would be the final time.

Fensterstock then erupted:

> Your Honor, may I ask for a recess, if not a mistrial. I have had it. There is nobody in this world, nobody in this world that is going to abuse me as I have been abused. I have had an unfair trial from the beginning of this....

Justice Loreto immediately declared a recess and invited to his chambers Judge Peck and Sidney Goldstein, who at the Court's request had been attending the trial for several days. I was not invited to attend, nor was Fensterstock. A record was made of the in camera session and of one that followed a few weeks later. To cut to the quick, Justice Loreto stated that he would no longer tolerate Fensterstock's behavior; the Port Authority would have to appoint other trial counsel. Rereading a half-century later the transcript of those sessions, I was astonished by the depth of Judge Peck's feelings, after having been subjected to week after week of Fensterstock's badgering and discourtesies.[6]

---

[6] I may appear to have dwelt unnecessarily on an adversary's trial tactics and demeanor, particularly to those who subscribe to the maxim "*De mortuis nihil nisi bonum*" ("Speak only well of the dead"). I can only respond that Fensterstock's repeated insinuations that Judge Peck was receiving favored treatment were (in Justice Loreto's words) "most offensive," "contemptuous," and (in Judge Peck's words) "conduct unbecoming a lawyer." In the end, Fensterstock landed on his feet. He left the Port Authority to become the first director of the newly established "Civil Appeals Management Plan" office of the U.S. Court of Appeals for the Second Circuit.

I recall conducting research to find another instance of a judge removing trial counsel without holding counsel in contempt or finding counsel guilty of some form of illegal conduct. I could not find any precedent for what had transpired in our case.

As successor counsel, the Port Authority turned to Whitney North Seymour, the senior litigation partner of Simpson, Thacher & Bartlett, to carry on with the trial. Seymour was as different from Fensterstock as day from night and a wise choice by the Port Authority to represent it. A lawyer with as many accomplishments as any I have met—he had been President of the American and New York City Bar Associations, as well as the American College of Trial Lawyers—Whitney Seymour cut an imposing figure; he was roughly six foot three and was as much a presence in court as was his good friend David Peck. Their courtroom styles, however, were very different: Judge Peck for all his formality and courtliness was a tenacious examiner of witnesses, whereas Whitney Seymour was laid-back and soft-spoken but in his very different way equally effective as an advocate.

I learned a valuable lesson from Whitney Seymour: although he was decades older and infinitely more accomplished than I, he was invariably courteous to me, as though the difference in our ages could not and should not conceal the fact that we were members of the same profession, "brothers at the bar." As the years have passed, I have always tried to behave toward younger lawyers with the same courtesy and respect that Whitney Seymour exhibited toward me. I hope that I have not failed, at least not often.

When the trial resumed, we concluded the buildings phase and then turned to the valuation of the Hudson Tubes, which presented a unique quandary: What was "just compensation," as mandated by the United States and New York

Constitutions, for a transit system that had not turned a profit for decades, yet was demonstrably indispensable to the economic well-being of New York City, had cost $62 million to construct at the turn of the century, and would have cost nearly $500 million to reproduce in 1965?

The unprofitability of the Hudson Tubes system had driven Hudson & Manhattan into bankruptcy reorganization, from which it had emerged only recently. (The transit system has continued to be unprofitable under the ownership of PATH. It was reported not long ago to have lost more than $300 million in a recent fiscal year.)

Reproduction was not a fantasy, for the existing alternate trans-Hudson facilities (the Lincoln and Holland vehicular tunnels, the rail tunnel to Penn Station, and the George Washington Bridge) could not absorb the Hudson Tubes passenger traffic—31,500,000 paying passengers in 1961—without massive and unacceptable delays. Even with due regard to the long-established principle that "value to the taker" could not be considered in establishing just compensation, it seemed to me and to others grossly unfair that Hudson & Manhattan should be awarded only the $2 million or so scrap value of the Hudson Tubes.

We introduced evidence portraying the laborious construction of the Hudson Tubes at the end of the nineteenth and beginning of the twentieth centuries and of the physical condition of the Hudson Tubes system.

We also engaged the engineering firm of Ford & Bacon to estimate the cost of reconstructing the system in 1962, the year of the Port Authority condemnation. The evidence of original and reproduction cost may have been tedious, but it was also meticulously assembled. We took pains not to exaggerate or inflate the costs. The Port Authority's sole challenge was that the evidence was irrelevant.

Hudson Tubes
Washington St. Northbound Tunnel

What was "just compensation" when the evidence in its totality pointed to almost diametrically opposed conclusions? Justice Loreto resolved this quandary in a thoughtful, well-reasoned opinion delivered in December 1965. He noted that the conventional formula of "market value" was inapplicable because there was no "market" for the Hudson Tubes. He observed that while the Port Authority experts had opined that the highest and best use and value of the Hudson Tubes was in liquidation, neither they nor "any responsible person" had suggested that it should be dismantled. The "exceptional circumstances of this case," Justice Loreto reasoned, "do not permit the application of any conventional legal formula."

Analogizing to "Newton's experiment with prisms showing that white light is composed of all the colors of the spectrum," Justice Loreto stated that "all the approaches to valuation entering into the informed mind and sensitive conscience of the court lend to an appropriate degree in the resulting decision." He awarded $55 million for the entire railroad, of which he allocated $30 million to the tunnels. Obviously aware that the amount he awarded as just compensation for the transit system would profoundly impact trading in the outstanding bonds, Judge Loreto had had his lengthy opinion typed and, just before issuing his decision, entered the amount of the award in ink.

Employing traditional condemnation techniques for valuing real property, Justice Loreto awarded $17,845,000 for the twin office buildings at 30 and 50 Church Street.

On appeal, the Appellate Division, dividing 3–2, reduced the award for the Hudson Tubes system from $55 million to $2.2 million, the system's scrap value. Each of the five Justices delivered an opinion, which was and remains unprecedented in my experience. Justice Stevens, whose opinion was delivered first, found the governing principle to be: "[W]hat has the owner lost for which it should be compensated?" Since the Hudson Tubes had been unprofitable for decades, the owner's only alternative to continued operation at a loss was to cease operations and scrap the physical facility. Hence, scrap value was "just compensation." Justice Breitel, who presided over the panel (and subsequently became Chief Judge of the New York Court of Appeals) and whose concurrence was necessary to the result, concurred "with great reluctance," "constrained… by the present authorities."

On our appeal to the New York Court of Appeals, the New York and New Jersey attorneys general weighed in on the Port Authority's side. In October 1967, the Court of Appeals reversed the Appellate Division over a lone dissent with Judge Breitel, who in the interim had been elevated to the Court of Appeals, not participating. Judge Burke, speaking for the majority, posed the question before the Court by asking whether it could be "said by any objective standard that an award of scrap value—*nothing* —is fair and just for the tunnel property, an essential part of an essential public facility…which with some minor expenditures, will function as good as new for an indefinite period?" Judge Burke answered that question: "We think not." Considering all the relevant factors, the Court of Appeals concluded that Justice Loreto's award of $30 million for the tunnels was "fair and just." As for the remainder of the transit system, the Court found that a remand was necessary because Justice Loreto had not adequately taken into account the physical and technological obsolescence of the property or the system's unprofitability.

The Court of Appeals decision noted that the Court was required by the bi-state legislation authorizing the condemnation to apply New Jersey law to the portion of the condemned property located in that state. Finding no New

Jersey cases dealing with even remotely comparable circumstances, the Court concluded that it was "not unreasonable to assume that the view we have taken would be adopted by" the New Jersey Supreme Court.

And so the roller-coaster continued: the trial court's award of $55 million, reduced to $2.2 million by the Appellate Division, became in the Court of Appeals $30 million plus an amount for the non-tunnel property to be determined on remand.

The Port Authority was not yet finished. It not only sought certiorari review[7] by the United States Supreme Court, but also tried to invoke the Supreme Court's original jurisdiction by manufacturing a dispute between the States of New York and New Jersey. The latter state moved for leave to file a complaint in the Supreme Court alleging that the decision of the New York Court of Appeals violated the compact creating the Port Authority. (I am willing to wager that the Port Authority's counsel participated in drafting the complaint.) On April 1, 1968, the certiorari petition and the motion for leave to file a complaint were both denied. On remand, we negotiated a settlement of $11 million for the non-tunnel property, resulting in a total railroad recovery of $41 million, exclusive of interest.

There was separate briefing on the appropriate rate of interest. The New York statutory rate at the time was 4 percent, far below prevailing market rates (as the current New York statutory 9 percent rate is far above market rates). Although I crafted an argument that application of the below-market statutory rate was unconstitutional, the argument was rejected by the courts.

[7] "Certiorari" is a writ or order by which a higher court exercises discretion to review a decision of a lower court.

* * *

With the Hudson & Manhattan case finally over, I was able to take an extended vacation for the first time in six years. My wife Ann and I rented a house on the north shore of the Caribbean island of Jamaica. We spent a great deal of time on the beach with our children, Jeff and Sarah, both of whom had been born during the pendency of the Hudson & Manhattan case. Indulging my passion for deep-sea fishing, I went out one day and was sitting on an elevated "fighting chair" when a tropical storm arose and the heavens opened. I sat there fully exposed and drenched to the skin, wondering what the hell I was doing there.

The storm eventually subsided, the sky cleared, and the large fish came up from the depths to feed. I hooked a blue marlin weighing about 200 pounds and after a forty-five-minute struggle managed to land the fish. During those forty-five minutes, the marlin strove with all its strength to resist. I can still see it breaching the surface and seeming almost to walk on the water. I have a photograph with the captain, the mate, and the magnificent fish. I appear in the photo to be holding the rod casually with my left elbow tucked into my side. In fact, I was so exhausted from fighting the marlin that I could not hold the rod without support. And when I returned to my car in the parking lot, I needed both hands to release the parking brake.

* * *

I look out the window in the office the firm generously provides me in retirement, and I see the new 1 World Trade Center looming like a colossus in the middle distance. I realize that I have viewed that site at five different stages of

MAC with blue marlin and crew

development over a half-century: first as two blocks of four-story multi-use structures and two twenty-story office buildings; then as a vacant construction site; then as the site of the 100-story Twin Towers, visible from miles away; then as a construction site again after the devastation of 9/11 (what an impersonal shorthand for a devastating tragedy!); and finally as the site of a new behemoth of a building again bearing the name "World Trade Center." I feel like the survivor of a half-century storm.

13

THE HUDSON & MANHATTAN FEE CASE

The Hudson & Manhattan saga did not end with the Port Authority's rebuff by the United States Supreme Court, but rather continued because Judge Peck was unable to agree with the client on our fee. The fee arrangement had been memorialized in a letter dated July 4, 1963, from Judge Peck to Hudson & Manhattan's new President, Walter T. Margetts, Jr. That letter, referring to an earlier conversation with Margetts' predecessor, recited an understanding that the firm "would bill quarterly on account on the basis of minimal time charges," with "the fixation of the final fee" to be

> agreed upon at the termination of the matter, the fee to be fixed in accordance with all the considerations appropriately entering into the fixation of the fee in such a matter, including the time spent, the nature and importance of the matter, the character and extent of the services rendered, and the resulting benefit to the corporation.

When that agreement proved impossible to reach, Hudson & Manhattan retained Simon Rifkind, a former federal judge and at the time the senior litigation partner of the Paul, Weiss firm, to try to resolve the dispute. I recall meeting with Judge Rifkind (as he was commonly addressed and referred to) in his large office to provide information about the condemnation proceeding. I endeavored to answer all his questions, and I believe I did so. (I am grateful for the opportunity to have met and talked with Judge Rifkind, truly a giant of the bar.)

Unfortunately, Judge Rifkind failed in his attempt to negotiate a settlement. Judge Peck then proposed to his former client that the parties invoke the little-known and rarely used Simplified Procedure for Court Determination of Disputes provided in Section 3031 of the New York Civil Practice Law and Rules. That procedure permits the commencement of an action by filing a statement, signed by all parties or their attorneys, "specifying plainly and concisely the claims and defenses between the parties and the relief requested." Walter Margetts agreed to the procedure and agreed also to have the dispute referred to Justice Loreto, who had presided over the condemnation proceeding and was as familiar as anyone other than Judge Peck and me with the services for which compensation was sought.

I recall the trial well. Every morning I would take the Erie Lackawanna train from Short Hills, New Jersey, to which my growing family (my wife Ann, children Jeff and Sarah, and a third child, Paul, about to be born) had moved four years earlier. At the Hoboken terminal, I would transfer—fittingly—to the PATH train. I would be met by a car at the Christopher Street station, pick up Bill Piel at his home on West 11th Street and then Judge Peck at his Park Avenue apartment, stop to pick up sandwiches at Poll's (a renowned Upper East Side delicatessen), and then drive to the Bronx County Courthouse, where the trial was conducted. On the way, Judge Peck would pull from his pocket scraps of paper on which he had written notes about the case in the middle of the night when he could not sleep. Each day, he, Bill Piel, and I would carry our bag of sandwiches to a small park across from the courthouse and simultaneously unwind from the morning in court and prepare for the afternoon's proceedings. The daily routine was unvarying and unforgettable.

Judge Peck testified for three full days. His memory of the

six-year-long condemnation proceeding was breathtakingly complete, and his testimony lucid and compelling. Essentially he delivered a monologue with an occasional question from Bill Piel to preserve the formal appearance of direct examination. I also testified, as did Jack Jaqua.

We called three expert witnesses: Bernard Bermant, a prominent member of the condemnation bar; Orison Marden, a senior partner of White & Case and, so far as I know, the only lawyer to have been President of the American, New York State, and New York City bar associations; and Bethuel Webster, senior partner of the Webster, Sheffield firm and also a former president of the New York City Bar Association.

When Hudson & Manhattan's turn came to present its case, it subpoenaed Judge Rifkind, its former counsel, who had been succeeded by Jim Oliensis of the Kaye, Scholer firm. The purpose of calling Judge Rifkind was to extract from him an opinion as to the value of our firm's services. I will never forget Judge Rifkind, a slight but sprightly man, standing in the well of the courtroom and asking permission to address the Court from there, rather than take the witness stand. Having received that permission, he then said that "it would be out of order, unseemly, and inappropriate for me to give testimony" because he had been retained by Hudson & Manhattan to recommend a settlement to both sides, and if that effort proved unsuccessful, his understanding with his client was that he "would depart from this matter and have nothing further to do with it and render no other service in connection with it." Justice Loreto, to whom we cited controlling authority that no one could be compelled to be an expert witness against his will, excused Judge Rifkind from the courtroom.

After hearing evidence for two weeks, Justice Loreto issued

a thirty-page opinion. Rereading it not long ago after nearly forty-five years, I was struck once again by the thoughtfulness, thoroughness, and judiciousness demonstrated by Justice Loreto. After all, this was a fee question, which would normally be resolved without extended consideration and expression. It was almost as though in the fee case Justice Loreto was reliving the underlying condemnation.

The opinion began by referring to "[t]he enormity of the task undertaken" and the "great uncertainty of the outcome." It then described Judge Peck's multiple responsibilities—direct examination and cross-examination of witnesses, finalizing all the written briefs, and delivery of the oral arguments—as having been "brilliantly performed." Gaining a reversal by the Court of the Appeals of the Appellate Division award of scrap value for the railroad was a "success… brilliantly plucked out of defeat." Justice Loreto also noted the uniqueness of the condemnation proceeding: "Nothing like [the Hudson Tubes] had ever before been the subject of condemnation." The proceeding "was unusual, it was unique in every sense of the word." In conclusion, Justice Loreto awarded our firm $3.3 million for services rendered regarding the railroad and $450,000 for services relating to the two office buildings—a total of $3.75 million, which was roughly $500,000 more than Judge Peck had offered to accept in settlement.

It is evident from his opinion that Justice Loreto took his responsibility for determining Sullivan & Cromwell's fee as seriously as he had the determination of "just compensation" in the condemnation proceeding. One last point should be made: Believing the condemnation proceeding to have been unique, even though he had devoted considerable time and thought to rendering his fee decision, Justice Loreto decided not to release his thirty-page opinion for publication. There is an appropriately self-effacing quality to that restraint, which I find remarkable and which reinforces my high opinion of him as a jurist.

The Appellate Division affirmed unanimously without opinion, as did the Court of Appeals (the latter court had previously granted leave to appeal, though "some of the members of the court believe[d] that the granting of leave [was] improvident upon the ground that there [was] no reviewable question presented").

I must recount one incident in the case that was a stroke of advocacy genius the likes of which I have never seen before or since. In his argument to Justice Loreto, Bill Piel noted that his adversary had focused almost exclusively on the hourly rate—more than $475 per hour (a princely hourly rate at the time for a lawyer's fee)—represented by the fee we were seeking for services rendered in the railroad case. Bill then held up a photocopy of an article in the *London Times* reporting on the 1878 trial of a notorious libel suit brought by the painter James Whistler against the highly regarded critic John Ruskin, who in reviewing an exhibition of Whistler's work had sneered at "the ill-educated conceit of the artist" that "nearly approached the aspect of willful imposture." Ruskin continued: "I…never expected to hear a coxcomb ask two hundred guineas for flinging a pot of paint in the public's face."

Unsurprisingly, Whistler sued Ruskin for libel. At the trial Ruskin's counsel asked Whistler on cross-examination how long it took him to finish one of his paintings. When Whistler replied that it took only a couple of days, Ruskin's counsel asked rhetorically whether two days of work was worth the 200 guineas Whistler wanted for the painting. Whistler famously replied: "No. I ask it for the knowledge I have gained in the work of a lifetime."

Bill Piel's analogy of Judge Peck's trial performance to the work of a great artist drawing upon the experience of a lifetime was nothing short of brilliant. To my mind, it effectively disposed of Hudson & Manhattan's dogged and formulaic reliance on hourly rates. I can visualize and hear Bill as clearly now as when I was sitting beside him forty-five years ago. I never learned where he had discovered the *London Times* report of Whistler's suit against Ruskin.

I cannot say for certain, but I believe that the fee received by Sullivan & Cromwell for representing Hudson & Manhattan and its rapid transit subsidiary, Hudson Rapid Tubes, was among the largest fees that had been received by the firm in its then-ninety-one-year history. The "Committee," which was and remains the governing body of the firm, celebrated the occasion by holding a dinner for its members and their spouses at Arthur Dean's splendid apartment at 10 Gracie Square. My wife Ann and I were invited. We were at least twenty-five years younger than anyone else present. At the end of the meal, the members of the Committee, then all men of course, repaired to the study for cognac and cigars. Not being certain what I was supposed to do, I joined them with some hesitation. I remember looking over my shoulder at Ann, who remained with the other spouses. She did not appear pleased at having been left behind, and looking back after more than four decades, I can understand why.

14

KLEIN V. SECURITIES CLEARANCE CORP.

This case is worthy of discussion only because it was the first jury trial in which I was participated as counsel. Indeed, it was the first jury trial I ever attended in any capacity!

* * *

One of the more colorful courthouse frequenters a half-century ago was Ernest Klein, a Hasidic rabbi who lived in Brooklyn and was a seemingly addicted securities trader. Rabbi Klein's MOS was to purchase stocks and bonds on the thinnest of margins. If the price of the stocks or bonds fell, his loan was called, and if he lacked the funds to pay the loan, the securities serving as collateral would be liquidated. Rabbi Klein would invariably sue, and when he lost, as he usually did, he would occasionally then sue the defendant's lawyers. One might say that he was a professional litigant as well as a seemingly obsessive securities trader.

In this case, Rabbi Klein had purchased bonds (and borrowed all but 3 percent of the purchase price) from Securities Clearance Corporation in 1958. Jerome Ackerman, a stockholder and director of Securities Clearance Corporation, repledged certain of the bonds to Belgian-American Banking Corporation to secure two loans made to him individually by Belgian-American. The bank believed Ackerman to be the owner of the securities and that it was entitled to hold the bonds until its loan to Ackerman was paid off.

Without going into unnecessary detail, in November 1958 Rabbi Klein was under-margined; Securities Clearance Corp. called its loan to him; and Ackerman instructed

Belgian-American to deliver the bonds to Hayden, Stone & Company, a now defunct brokerage firm. The bank did so, and when Rabbi Klein was unable to redeem the bonds, he sued Securities Clearance Corp., Ackerman and Belgian-American, which retained Sullivan & Cromwell as counsel.

Rabbi Klein demanded a jury, and the case eventually went to trial in April 1966 before Justice Thomas Aurelio of the Supreme Court, New York County. I was lead counsel for the bank, and Mike Maney, an extraordinarily able junior associate who went on to become a partner, assisted me. I was surprised at the time, and remain so today, that the firm would entrust a jury trial to a sixth-year associate who had never before tried a case to a jury either as lead counsel or even as second chair. I can only surmise that Judge Peck, with whom I had tried the Hudson & Manhattan condemnation case, had assured our litigation partners that I was up to the challenge, for which I was and remain grateful to him.

During the trial, I took pains to be courteous and, to the extent it was appropriate, friendly toward Rabbi Klein in the hallway outside the courtroom during recesses. The last thing I needed was for Rabbi Klein to sue me or, worse yet, Sullivan & Cromwell if he lost.

At the close of plaintiff's case, after the accumulation of more than seven hundred pages of testimony and the receipt in evidence of forty-five exhibits, Justice Aurelio granted defendants' motion for judgment. He recited several conclusions, including that neither plaintiff nor anyone acting on his behalf had made a proper legal tender for the bonds and that plaintiff was under-margined and had failed, after due notice, to bring the margin up to the amount required under his agreement. Never one to leave the field if another battle could be fought, Rabbi Klein appealed. The

Appellate Division affirmed the judgment for defendants unanimously without opinion, and the Court of Appeals denied leave to appeal.

POSTSCRIPT: Neither Sullivan & Cromwell nor I was sued by Rabbi Klein.

15

LEFKOWITZ V. CORNELL UNIVERSITY

The spring and summer of 1968 were a time of intense student unrest provoked by the Vietnam War. The Kent State killings left a searing impression on the American consciousness. The unrest invaded the Ithaca campus of Cornell. I vividly recall an image of an African-American student wearing a bandolier of bullets marching in protest on the campus.

The unrest in Ithaca focused on a University-owned facility that was not widely known: the Cornell Aeronautical Laboratory located in the Buffalo suburb of Cheektowaga. The Laboratory had been given by Curtiss-Wright Corporation to Cornell in December 1945 shortly after the end of World War II. Perhaps because of its distance from all other parts of Cornell, the Laboratory operated with considerable autonomy, which was just the way the scientists working there liked it.

Over time, the Cornell Aeronautical Laboratory developed the automatic seatbelt and the crash test dummy. By 1968 the Laboratory had grown from roughly 500 to 1,475 employees. It became a focus for intense student unrest because it had a contract with the U.S. military to refine napalm, which our soldiers fired with devastating effects not only on Vietcong bunkers but also on Vietnamese villages. The University Administration and Board of Trustees decided that the wisest course for the University would be to sell the Laboratory. Enter on the scene EDP Technology Corporation, which offered to acquire the Laboratory for $25 million. To put that amount in perspective, the University's total endowment at the time was approximately $175 million.

The Laboratory scientists were less than thrilled at the prospect of working for a profit-oriented and cost-conscious corporation rather than for the University, which had held a relatively loose rein over the Laboratory's operations. They somehow prevailed on New York Attorney General Louis Lefkowitz to bring suit to enjoin the sale of the Laboratory to ESB on the ground that Cornell owned the Laboratory "for public trust purposes" that would be violated by a sale to a profit-oriented private business enterprise. The complaint sought an injunction prohibiting the sale.

The University turned to Sullivan & Cromwell for representation. It was natural that Cornell should do so, for (as I've mentioned) the firm's chairman, Arthur H. Dean, not only was a Cornell alumnus, but also had recently been chair of its board of trustees for a decade. Bob McDonald, head of the firm's Tax Department and also a Cornell alumnus, had spearheaded the firm's representation of the University in many matters and did so in this instance.

Bob McDonald was a tall man, then in his mid-fifties, with craggy features. His mind was sharp as a razor, and he had an impish and infectious sense of humor. His greatest asset, perhaps, was his wife Kay, who at the time was an attorney in the Legal Aid Society's Juvenile Rights Division. Kay went on to become a judge and ultimately the Presiding Judge of the Family Court in Manhattan, where she instituted several significant reforms. There was not a more engaging, delightful, and yet professionally committed couple than Bob and Kay McDonald.

I was a thirty-two-year-old fledgling litigation partner when Bob McDonald asked me to take charge of our defense of Cornell. Because the case had a distinctly local flair, we engaged as co-counsel the Phillips, Lytle firm in Buffalo, and in particular its partner Alexander ("Sandy") Cordes. I signed up one of our junior litigation associates, Scott Romney, to work with me. The family name is, of course, well-known. Scott's father, George Romney, was a longtime president of American Motors Corporation and then Governor of Michigan, and his brother Mitt became the Republican presidential nominee in 2012. Scott left the firm not long only after this case. I understood he was going to Utah to develop a ski resort, but the last time I saw his name, he was a partner in one of the premier Detroit law firms. I guess his personal journey eventually led him back to his hometown.

The Cornell Aeronautical Laboratory case was tried in Erie County Supreme Court in the winter. If you have never spent time in Buffalo in December, you are fortunate. The wind roars in off Lake Erie, often accompanied by snow. The wind can be so fierce that the city is (or at least was) occasionally compelled to string a hawser for pedestrians to hold onto when they try to cross the street.

Scott Romney was an able associate and an observant Mormon. He did not drink, smoke, or swear, three vices—or virtues, according to one's point of view—that helped me "make it through the night," as the song goes, that December in Buffalo. As though his abstinence from the vices I enjoyed were not enough, Scott would go for a run each morning in the frigid cold, even though he suffered from asthma.

The trial was memorable for me, not just because of the historical interest of its subject matter, but also because it exposed me to perhaps the greatest trial lawyer—certainly one of the five finest—I have encountered in my professional life: Frank Raichle, who represented the prospective purchaser, ESB Corporation. By this point in his career, Frank, who was seventy-two and spoke with a slight tremor, had achieved almost mythical status in the profession. He had represented one of the principal defendants in the notorious Appalachian mafia criminal prosecution in the '50s. He was also an early president of the American College of Trial Lawyers.

Frank Raichle had a way of commanding the attention of everyone in the courtroom when it suited his purpose. I remember one moment when a Laboratory scientist was giving testimony that was damaging to our side. Frank stood up, moved his chair about two feet to the right, and sat down again. When he stood, all eyes in the courtroom turned to him, and the spell of the witness's testimony was irretrievably broken.

On another occasion, Frank cross-examined one of the Laboratory scientists, who had analogized in his testimony to the effect a burr would have under the saddle on a horse. Frank asked on cross-examination whether it truly required a PhD to determine the effect a burr would have if placed under the saddle on a horse. The entire courtroom was reduced to hysterical laughter. Frank Raichle was truly a gifted artist, and the courtroom his canvas.

It was clear from the instrument of gift executed by Curtiss-Wright, as well as documents executed contemporaneously by Cornell, that there were no restrictions on the gift. To prove the negative irrefutably (we thought), we were able to locate the lawyer who had represented Curtiss-Wright in making the gift and had in fact shaped the entire transaction. He testified that far from seeking to impose a restriction on the gift of the Laboratory, he had advised his client that it was imperative that the gift be "absolutely unconditional."

After the trial and after both sides had proposed findings of fact and conclusions of law, Justice Kelly rendered his decision in March 1970. Having posed the crucial question as whether the gift of the Laboratory by Curtiss-Wright to Cornell was "a 'public trust' with a restricted purpose which will prevent the sale of the Laboratory to EDP," Justice Kelly held that "Cornell itself understood that...there was an obligation to continue to operate the laboratory as a research facility for the public benefit." No matter that neither the gift instruments nor Cornell's acknowledgment thereof contained any words of limitation or restriction. The "evidence relating to the circumstances surrounding the gift" established that "a charitable trust" was created.

On appeal, the Appellate Division, Fourth Department, unanimously reversed. Acknowledging that Cornell and the Laboratory had made statements over the years that the Laboratory would be operated as "an instrument of service to the aircraft industry, to education, and to the public at large," the Appellate Division nevertheless observed that in none of Curtiss-Wright's letters at the time of the gift was it "stated that the gifts were conditioned upon Cornell's perpetual operation of the laboratory" and that "mere expressions of Cornell's then present and contemplated future policies with respect to the operation of the laboratory" did not constitute steps by Cornell "to impose upon itself the legal obligations" to adhere to such policies. The sole limitation upon the University was that if it were to sell the Laboratory, "it use the proceeds of the sale for the 'advancement of science and education'." For these reasons the Appellate Division reversed the trial court and ordered the Attorney General's complaint dismissed. The Attorney General appealed to the Court of Appeals, which unanimously affirmed the Appellate Division without troubling to write an opinion.

Unfortunately, by the time the Court of Appeals ruled in 1971, the contract between EDP and Cornell had expired, and, as Cornell stated publicly, it was "mutually agreed" that the completion date would not be extended. It was my understanding at the time that EDP was not in good financial condition and could not perform the contract, which had provided for EDP to pay one-half the purchase price in bonds that would have had little value to Cornell. In short, the transaction was never consummated.

In 1972 Cornell reorganized the Laboratory as a for-profit corporation and sold its stock to the public.

16

CLARK OIL V. INTERPROVINCIAL AND LAKEHEAD PIPELINES

None of my colleagues, to the best of my knowledge, has appeared before the Interstate Commerce Commission, nor can I recall any litigation in the firm focused on an Executive Agreement between the United States and another sovereign country. The proceeding I am about to describe had both unusual features.

* * *

In 1968 Sullivan & Cromwell was retained by Interprovincial Pipeline Co. of Canada ("Interprovincial") and its U.S. subsidiary, Lakehead Pipeline Co. ("Lakehead"), to defend against a complaint filed with the Interstate Commerce Commission by Clark Oil & Refining Corporation ("Clark"), which operated two refineries in the Chicago area. Clark sought an order directing Interprovincial and Lakehead to file a tariff for the transportation of crude oil from Alberta to Clark's Illinois refineries.

Interprovincial operated the longest pipeline in the Western Hemisphere, extending about 2,000 miles from Alberta, entering the United States at the North Dakota boundary and continuing through Minnesota, northern Wisconsin, and the upper Michigan peninsula across the Straits of Mackinac and through the lower Michigan peninsula to the international boundary at a point near the twin cities of Port Huron, Michigan, and Sarnia, Ontario. In order to increase system capacity, a second or "loop" line was constructed between Superior, Wisconsin, and Sarnia. The route chosen for the loop line passed near Chicago, both to avoid the costly construction of a second crossing of the Straits of Mackinac and to take advantage of a route passing through the highly industrialized area south of Lake Michigan.

Pipeline crossings of an international boundary of the United States are covered by permits issued by the Secretary of State. As a condition of granting a permit for the Interprovincial loop line, the State Department exacted a commitment from the Canadian government, Interprovincial, and Lakehead that no oil would be shipped into the Chicago area prior to January 1, 1970. The prohibition on deliveries in the Chicago area was undoubtedly designed to protect pipelines bringing oil north to Chicago from the area adjacent to the Gulf Coast.

The agreement was expressed in diplomatic "notes" dated September 25, 1967, exchanged between the Canadian Ambassador to the United States and the Acting U.S. Secretary of State. Restricted by this agreement, Interprovincial and Lakehead had no alternative but to decline Clark's request for a tariff. Clark proceeded to file a complaint with the Interstate Commerce Commission, contending that Lakehead was required as a common carrier to accede to Clark's demand for the delivery of oil.

Lakehead answered the complaint, while Interprovincial moved to dismiss on the ground that, as a Canadian corporation doing business solely within Canada, it was not subject to the jurisdiction of the ICC or to the provisions of the Interstate Commerce Act. Interprovincial coupled that motion with a request that decision of the motion be deferred until after adjudication of the claim against Lakehead, arguing that if the ICC decided against Clark, no relief would be granted against either Lakehead or Interprovincial, whereas if the Commission ruled in Clark's favor, Clark had agreed that relief would be granted against Lakehead alone.

The matter was assigned to a hearing examiner, and the parties filed briefs. Clark's basic contention was that the statutory obligation of Lakehead as a "common carrier" to file a tariff and to provide transportation overrode the "secret intergovernmental notes," which in any event, Clark argued, were invalid in the absence of congressional authorization for the Executive to regulate foreign commerce in this manner. In response, we argued on Lakehead's behalf that the diplomatic notes had the solemnity of an Executive Agreement and constituted a valid exercise of the authority granted to the President by the Trade Expansion Act of 1962.

On September 9, 1969, the Hearing Examiner issued a report and order dismissing the complaint. He ruled that the exchange of diplomatic notes "[bore] the dignity similar to that of a treaty" and that "a treaty takes precedence over the provisions of a statute…in the event of an irreconcilable conflict between the two." For that proposition, the sole authority cited by the Hearing Examiner was a 100-year-old United States Supreme Court decision, which struck me at the time, and on again rereading recently, as a weak precedent.

Clark asked the full ICC or a division thereof to review the Hearing Examiner's report and order, and on October 9, 1969, filed its supporting brief, to which we responded twenty days later. Bear in mind that the clock was ticking: the prohibition imposed by the Executive Agreement was set to expire January 1, 1970. When the ICC failed to render a decision by that date, we filed a motion on Lakehead's behalf on January 8, 1970, asking that the proceeding be dismissed as moot. A hearing was held before the full Commission on January 21, 1970, by which date Lakehead had filed a tariff and was delivering oil to Clark. On March 19, 1970, the Commission issued a brief report and order granting our motion and dismissing the proceeding as moot.

My description of this proceeding might suggest that it was one of the drier, less interesting matters on which I have worked. In fact, it was quite memorable for two reasons.

First, if the proscription on deliveries to the Chicago area had not expired by its terms, the conflict posed between the duty of common carriers under the Interstate Commerce Act to provide transportation, on the one hand, and the contrary prohibition of the Executive Agreement, on the other, was unprecedented (notwithstanding the 100-year-old inapposite decision cited by the Hearing Examiner) and, therefore, an appealing subject for a grant of certiorari and review by the Supreme Court. Indeed, this was the most "cert-worthy" case I have ever worked on.

Second, my adversaries—Paul Porter, Jim McAlee, and Alex Bennett of Arnold & Porter—were among both the ablest and the most congenial of all the adversaries with whom I have crossed swords over the decades. Their briefs were articulate and persuasive, as was their oral advocacy. Paul Porter was larger than life and a widely known Washington persona; he had been Chairman of the Federal Communications Commission, Deputy Administrator of the Office of Price Administration, and a senior diplomat. Porter was gracious personally, a truly superb advocate, and a delightful raconteur.

I still recall forty-five years later one of his stories. How, he asked, is the State Department like an elephant? In three ways, he answered: First, anything of significance occurs at very high places; second, it is invariably accompanied by much trumpeting and snorting; and, third, it takes many, many months to see the outcome. I hope you can see why I took a shine to Paul Porter.

17

ANTIDUMPING PROCEEDINGS (KMW AND AVESTA)

For the most part my life as an advocate has been blissfully free of administrative proceedings with their frequently arcane and tortuous procedures. In the early '70s, however, I participated in two proceedings before the Tariff Commission (now the International Trade Commission) under the Antidumping Act, which prohibits a foreign person from charging a lower price for a product sold into the United States than is charged for the same product in that person's home market, if the sale at less than fair value injures a domestic seller of the same product. Both proceedings involved affiliates of Axel Johnson & Co., a Swedish conglomerate that had been a client of Sullivan & Cromwell for many years. The affiliates in question were Karlstads Mekaniska Werkstad (KMW), which made papermaking machinery, and Avesta Jernwerks (Avesta), a steel producer.

* * *

KMW had sold two very large papermaking machines to Weyerhauser; one of the machines produced linerboard and the other corrugated paper. At the time, there were only two domestic producers of papermaking machines in the United States, Black-Clawson and Beloit. They jointly filed a formal complaint with the Treasury Department, which investigated their charges of violation of the Antidumping Act. In due course—"due course" consisting of seemingly endless submissions of data and argumentative letters—the Treasury Department determined that "an entire papermaking machine" (the linerboard machine) had been sold in the

United States at less than the "home market" price. Treasury then referred the matter to the Tariff Commission to determine whether an industry in the United States was being or was likely to be injured by the less-than-fair-value sale.

The machines sold by KMW to Weyerhauser had been assembled in Valiant, Oklahoma, near forest land owned by Weyerhauser. To learn more about the linerboard machine, I traveled to Valiant, which was no mean feat. I flew to Little Rock, drove to Texarkana, where I briefly visited the wife of my law school classmate Richard Arnold, and then drove a considerable distance to the one motel in Valiant, at which I arrived mid-evening. By then exhausted, I asked the motel receptionist whether there was anyplace nearby where I could get something quick to eat, to which she replied with a wink that there was a small establishment up the road where "you can get anything you want." I chose to go directly to my room and to bed—by myself.

I also traveled to Karlstad, Sweden, to examine KMW's manufacturing facilities and talk to officials to learn their export practices. Karlstad is a relatively small town with a tiny "airport" containing a single runway. I flew there from Stockholm in a single-engine prop plane. When we reached Karlstad, there was zero visibility. The pilot started flying in a crisscross pattern trying to pick up a signal from the shack that substituted for a terminal. I had never before, and have never since, been so frightened while flying.

Papermaking is not very high-tech. Pulp containing water and wood fiber is transformed into paper using three processes: compression by rollers, heat, and suction. In the case of the linerboard machine purchased by Weyerhauser from KMW, thousands of gallons of pulp per minute entered the machine at one end, and paper emerged in continuous rolls at the other.

The machine was truly enormous—imagine a single piece of equipment the length of two football fields—and the notion that anything truly comparable had been manufactured in the United States or for that matter anywhere in the world was almost laughable. But how was I going to convey that enormity and incomparability to the Tariff Commission? I asked whether there was a model of the machine and was told there was none. There was, however, a scale drawing about 15 feet long and 3 feet high that I could borrow.

I then faced a second quandary: how was I going to display the drawing? I couldn't simply hold one end while one of my colleagues stood holding the other 15 feet away; the drawing would either sag or tear. I finally lit on the idea of wrapping the drawing around two Torah scrolls, each of which would be held by a colleague. As I described the machine and the sequential steps in the papermaking process to the members of the Tariff Commission, my colleagues Mike Winger and Roger Chesley unrolled the drawing to display visually the part of the papermaking process that I was describing at the moment. And it worked! After a two-day hearing, the Tariff Commission determined that no domestic industry was or was likely to be injured by imports of papermaking machinery from Sweden.

One last footnote: my adversary in the KMW matter was an old Washington hand named Eugene Stewart, who was Executive Director of the Pulp and Paper Machinery Manufacturers' Association. Stewart was an unpleasant adversary: dismissive and mannered. But he could be drily humorous at times. When he entered the hearing room one morning, the Secretary of the Tariff Commission greeted him and asked in a friendly tone: "How are you today, Mr. Stewart?" Without skipping a beat, Stewart replied: "That, madam, is a question to which there is no felicitous reply."

* * *

In the same year as the papermaking machinery proceeding, I represented another Axel Johnson subsidiary, Avesta Jernverks, a stainless-steel plate, sheet, and strip producer, which was charged, along with three other Swedish steel mills, with having sold stainless-steel plate into the United States below the Swedish home market price and thereby injured domestic producers. As in the papermaking machinery matter, the Treasury Department made a finding of sales at less than fair value and injury, and the matter was referred to the Tariff Commission.

I arranged to visit the Avesta headquarters and took an overnight SAS flight from JFK to Stockholm accompanied by Borje Walhstrom, an Avesta executive. I fell asleep but was awakened by a seemingly celestial choir of song. When I opened my eyes, I saw three beautiful blonde young women dressed in white gowns walking slowly down the aisle, holding lit candles and singing the Neapolitan ballad "Santa Lucia." I said, as much to myself as to Borje: "I must have died and gone to heaven." He replied (in substance): "Are you ready as a lawyer to defend your right to be there?" I learned the next day that it was traditional in Sweden for women and girls to dress in white on the eve of the winter solstice and to walk the streets from house to house throughout the country, asking for alms for the poor. What a lovely custom! I have difficulty imagining it being replicated in the United States.

In Stockholm, I was treated to another delightful Swedish custom: sessions in a sauna alternating with dips in a cold pool. We took cold beers into the sauna. Four sauna/cold plunge cycles and two beers left you feeling not only purged but ready for a nap.

In the Tariff Commission proceeding that followed the

Treasury Department finding, I learned how different an administrative hearing could be from one in a court of law. While I was cross-examining a U.S. steel industry executive, I asked him a question which he flat-out refused to answer. I turned to the Chair of the Tariff Commission (a former congresswoman from Oregon) and respectfully requested that she direct the witness to answer my question. She replied in substance with a pained look on her face: "Mr. Cooper, if the witness won't answer the question, what can I do?"

We argued that imports of steel plate from Sweden could not be found to have injured or threatened to injure U.S. plate producers because during the six-month period in which the Treasury Department found sales of Swedish steel plate to have been made into the United States at less than fair value, domestic producers had increased their plate shipments by 30 percent over the preceding six-month period. Their profits had ceased to decline and, for at least one of the companies, had in fact increased. We also pointed out that for the thicknesses of steel plate in question, there was virtually no Swedish home market to serve as a basis for comparison.

Unfortunately, our arguments proved unavailing, and, in contrast to the papermaking machinery case, the Tariff Commission made a finding that the domestic stainless-steel plate industry had been injured by less-than-fair-value imports and imposed special antidumping duties. The Commission's statement of reasons supporting its decision consumed all of five pages and contained no discussion of the evidence at all.

Other than Mike Winger and Roger Chesley, the now-departed associates who worked with me on the KMW and Avesta proceedings, I know of no other Sullivan & Cromwell lawyer who has had a matter under the Antidumping Act during my years at the firm. All things considered, I'm not sure I can call that experience a badge of honor.

18

KENNECOTT COPPER AND CHASE BRASS

Triangle Industries, a brass mill fabricator principally of wire and cable products, filed a complaint in federal court in the Eastern District of Pennsylvania in June 1970 alleging that the three major copper producers—our client Kennecott, Anaconda, and Phelps Dodge—had conspired to increase the price of copper while failing to reflect those increases in the prices their subsidiaries charged for fabricated brass products. "Independent" fabricators like Triangle were thus "subjected…to a price squeeze." In October 1970 Reading Industries, a brass mill tube and pipe fabricator represented by the same firm that represented Triangle, filed a complaint in the Eastern District of Pennsylvania containing similar allegations.

The Triangle and Reading actions were spawned by a criminal antitrust indictment returned in the District of Connecticut several years earlier. The investigation culminating in that indictment, to which I have already alluded, had commenced in 1961. The indicted brass mill companies included Chase Brass, a subsidiary of Kennecott. Chase eventually pleaded nolo contendere, as did the other brass mill companies.

Fast-forward to the Triangle and Reading actions. The defendants moved to transfer both actions from the Eastern District of Pennsylvania to the Southern District of New York, invoking a federal statute authorizing an inter-district transfer "for the convenience of parties and witnesses" and "in the interest of justice…." Although New York City, where the three copper producer defendants maintained their principal offices, was only 90 miles distant from Philadelphia and within the range of compulsion by subpoenas issued out of the Eastern District of Pennsylvania, the judge presiding over both actions granted the transfer motions, observing wryly that "the only substantial connection between these actions and the Eastern District of Pennsylvania is that plaintiffs' counsel maintains his office here."

By the time these actions were commenced, I had become a partner, and Bill Piel handed over to me the primary responsibility for defending Kennecott and Chase. Phelps Dodge was represented by the Debevoise firm and Anaconda by Chadbourne. Plaintiffs' counsel was Harold Kohn, who had made his reputation as a plaintiff's treble-damage antitrust lawyer in the electrical equipment antitrust cases. Kohn was a formidable courtroom advocate. He had three lawyers assisting him: Jerry Cohen, low-key, amiable, and effective; Aaron Fine, a very impressive lawyer with an unimpressive exterior, who looked as though he had just emerged from a secondhand-clothing store; and Michael Hausfeld, a miniature version of his senior partner, very self-assured and equally abrasive.

Discovery proceeded over the next few years under the watchful eye of Southern District of New York Judge Morris Lasker, one of the most sensible and clear-thinking judges before whom I have appeared. We were appropriately forthcoming in producing documents and answering interrogatories; plaintiffs were not, or so it appeared to me.

One moment in the discovery process stands out vividly in my memory. During the deposition of an Anaconda executive by Hausfeld, he showed the witness a document produced by Anaconda in discovery that was clearly privileged and equally clearly had been produced inadvertently. Paul Pennoyer, the senior Chadbourne partner representing Anaconda, objected and demanded that the document and all copies in plaintiffs' possession be returned. Paul, a scion of the JP Morgan family, was tall and, even in his sixties, muscular. He had the largest hands of anyone I've ever known and, I was told many years later, had been the stroke on the Harvard crew. When Hausfeld declined, with a smirk, to return the document, Paul rose from his chair and strode to the other side of the table where Hausfeld sat. For a moment I thought Paul was going to throttle Hausfeld. Instead, he ripped the document from Hausfeld's hand. Hausfeld, visibly shaken, objected in a strained voice, but wisely chose not to pursue his objection.

After six years of discovery, plaintiffs' counsel proposed that the Reading action be tried first, and discovery thenceforth focused on its claims. In a Statement of Contentions filed at the Court's direction in September 1977, Reading abandoned the high-priced refined copper conspiracy claims of its complaint, reversed course 180 degrees, and substituted a new and contradictory theory: that (1) defendants had conspired to charge "artificially low" prices for refined copper; (2) those low prices, through a series of complex market interactions, had driven up the price of copper on the London Metal Exchange; and (3) because there was a "direct correlation" between the LME refined copper price and the price of copper scrap, which constituted Reading's principal copper input, Reading was compelled to pay higher scrap prices. If the reader has trouble following the economic logic of this skein of argument, be comforted that we had the same difficulty forty years ago.

After a series of depositions, during which two of Reading's experts conceded that the fabricated copper product markets had been "competitive" during the years in question, Reading formally withdrew its claims of violation and injury in the fabricated product markets, whereupon defendants moved for summary judgment. In a closely reasoned, lengthy opinion, Judge Lasker granted the motion on the ground that Reading lacked standing to pursue a claim that low-priced copper in the U.S. had caused high scrap prices on the LME. The Court of Appeals affirmed, agreeing with Judge Lasker that "the causal relationship between defendants' alleged violation and Reading's payment of high scrap prices is too remote to permit the imposition of liability." The Supreme Court denied certiorari, and after eleven years the Reading action finally ended.

Triangle's suit remained. As had Reading, Triangle sought to reverse course, moving to amend its complaint to substitute for its original "price-squeeze" claim a claim that defendants had reflected in their fabricated product prices the cost of refined copper they produced but not the cost of incremental copper supplies obtained from outside sources. Judge Lasker denied the motion to amend, reasoning that "it would not be in the interest of justice to permit amendments which alter, if they do not indeed contradict, previous claims, and which consequently prejudice the defendants by requiring them, eleven years after the complaint was filed, to defend against new claims."

In further discovery, Triangle sought in interrogatory answers to pursue the very claims the District Court had rejected in denying the motion to amend and abandoned all claims based on the previously pleaded conspiracy to raise the price of refined copper. Defendants thereupon moved for summary judgment. In opposing the motion, Triangle was required by a District Court "local" rule to specify each supposedly genuinely contested issue of material fact. Reviewing those issues one by one, Judge Lasker concluded that each involved (1) matters as to which Triangle's latest statement of position was "undercut" by contradictory admissions, (2) undisputed but irrelevant contentions, or (3) claims of injury for which a predicate basis for liability had not been shown. Judge Lasker thus saw through each of Triangle's obfuscating contentions and granted our summary judgment motion.

On appeal, the Court of Appeals, in a memorandum decision not thought by the panel to be worthy of formal publication, affirmed both the grant of summary judgment and the earlier denial of Triangle's motion to amend. The Court found that there was no justification for Triangle's "extraordinary delay" in seeking to amend its complaint and that the delay "threatened prejudice to defendants…." The Court affirmed Judge Lasker's grant of summary judgment because Triangle had "abandoned and expressly repudiated the claims asserted in its original complaint."

Rule 1 of the Federal Rules of Civil Procedure commands that those rules be administered to secure the "just, speedy and inexpensive" determination of disputes. The resolution of Reading's and Triangle's claims was "just," I believe, but it was surely neither "speedy" nor "inexpensive." When the copper and brass antitrust wars began in the spring of 1961, I was in my first year at Sullivan & Cromwell, single and unattached. When they ended in 1984, I was the managing partner of the firm's litigation group, married and the father of a son approaching his twentieth birthday and two other children.

Paul, Sarah and Jeff Cooper
(Photo by Peter Simon)

19

JURY TRIALS IN THE '80S

Esso Resources Canada Ltd. v. Hanover Insurance Co.

Casualty insurance coverage is typically provided for each "occurrence." Whether the events giving rise to an insurance claim constitute one occurrence or two can thus determine whether the insured receives a single or double recovery. That was the only seriously disputed issue in a 1984 jury trial in which I represented Esso Resources Canada Limited ("Esso Resources") suing Hanover Insurance Company and Utica Mutual Insurance Company in the Southern District of New York.

The case involved the Granduc copper mine owned by Newmont Mines Limited ("Newmont") in Tide Lake, British Columbia, an area not far from a place which, according to the *Guinness Book of World Records*, had the heaviest snowfall on the planet—as much as 100 feet a year.

Because of the depth of the annual snowfall, the mine concentrator facility, fifteen stories high at its highest point, was designed with a roof slanted at a 30-degree angle. The design engineers proceeded on the plausible theory that the heat generated by the concentrator operations would melt the snow sufficiently to create a film of water that would permit the snow to slide off the roof. Further, and I am now quoting from Judge Miner's majority opinion in the Second Circuit, "[d]ue to the size of the concentrator, structural design principles required that an expansion joint be installed in the middle of the building to permit expansion and contraction to occur without causing damage. Consequently the concentrator was designed as two adjacent structures…separated in the middle by a double set of columns."

All went well from the opening of the mine in 1970 till 1978 when, because of depressed copper prices, Newmont shut down the mine. Soon thereafter Newmont entered into negotiations to sell the mine to Esso Resources. While the negotiations were ongoing, Newmont discovered during an inspection of the mine property by helicopter on March 14, 1979, that a large section of the concentrator roof above the midline had collapsed, undoubtedly due to the accumulation of snow because the concentrator was no longer operating, its roof was not heated, and therefore snow did not slide off the roof. Three days later, while Newmont representatives were on-site, a large section of the roof below the midline also collapsed under the weight of snow.

The negotiations between Newmont and Esso Resources continued, and one month after the second collapse, they entered into an agreement under which Esso Resources agreed to purchase the mine property, and Newmont agreed to pursue insurance claims and hold in trust for Esso Resources 85 percent of any net insurance recovery. Esso Resources proceeded to repair the property at a total cost of approximately $6.6 million (Canadian).

Newmont settled with two of its insurers, including the excess insurance carrier, but two other insurers—Hanover, which covered 50 percent of the first $500,000 for any one "occurrence," and Utica, which provided intermediate coverage of $1 million in excess of $525,000, for any one "occurrence"—declined to settle, and Esso Resources and Newmont jointly sued those two insurers.

One of the challenges at trial was to convey to the jury an appreciation of the size and design of the concentrator. Fortunately (and unlike the KMW antidumping proceeding described above), there was a scale model, which we were able to use to good effect with our principal engineering witness, the Chief Engineer of Swan Wooster Engineering, the firm that had designed the concentrator. The jury members gathered around the model as the witness explained the design features adopted to deal with snow accumulation.

The Esso Resources case was tried to a jury in the Southern District of New York before Judge John Sprizzo, who had been appointed to the bench three or four years earlier after having been for many years the "law man" for his well-known partner Peter Fleming. Judge Sprizzo had an injudicious habit, whether intentional or not, of letting the jury know how he felt about the testimony of individual witnesses. If he found the testimony of a witness credible, he would lean forward in his chair exhibiting keen interest. If he was bored or found the testimony of a witness unworthy of belief, he would turn in his swivel chair so that his back was to the witness. That unfortunate habit aside, Judge Sprizzo was effective in presiding and fully grasped the nuances of the applicable law.

There were two principal questions for the jury to determine. The first issue was whether the temporary cessation of mine operations had constituted a "material change in the risk" of which the insurers should have been, but were not, notified. The second issue was whether the collapses had constituted one "occurrence" or two within the meaning of the policies. The jury deliberated for a little over two hours. While they did so, my partner Bill Dallas engaged Judge Sprizzo in chatter about horseracing, to which they were both devoted. (Judge Sprizzo had been seen at Belmont racetrack wearing a T-shirt with "Here Come Da Judge" emblazoned on the front.) I nervously paced back and forth, unable to concentrate on their banter about "split" times on the track and other arcane racing matters.

When the jury returned to render their verdict, they

answered specific questions that had been put to them. The jury found that there had not been a material change in the risk of which the defendant insurers had not been notified (Reader: please forgive the double negative), and further found that the collapses constituted two separate "occurrences," thereby doubling the liability of Hanover and Utica.

A third issue, determined by the Court, not the jury, was whether the recoverable amount should be converted from Canadian into U.S. dollars as of the date of breach or the date of the judgment. Judge Sprizzo held that the so-called "breach-day" rule should be applied, as we had argued, and his ruling was affirmed on appeal.

On appeal, the Second Circuit affirmed, with Judge Miner authoring an opinion in which Judge Newman joined. On the first issue, the Court majority held there was ample evidence from which a jury could find that Hanover and Utica agreed to insure the Granduc mine "without regard to the snow removal procedures being used or whether the building was heated." As to the number of occurrences, the Court held that Judge Sprizzo's charge to the jury correctly stated the law when he described their task as being to determine whether the loss was "the result of a single, continuous event or incident" or "separate events or incidents...." The Court further concluded that the jury finding of two occurrences was supported by the evidence.

Judge Van Graafeiland dissented vigorously, stating that the jury's finding that there had not been a material change in the risk "defie[d] all sense and logic, [was] completely without support in the evidence, and has resulted in a miscarriage of justice."

I learned a lesson in voir dire in the Esso Resources case. (*Voir dire* is an old Latin-derived French phrase meaning "to speak the truth" that is used to describe the preliminary examination of prospective jurors to determine their qualifications and suitability to serve.) One member of the jury venire (another Old French term referring to the group of citizens receiving a jury summons from whom a panel is selected to try a case), who was dressed in a casual T-shirt, described his occupation as being the erection of displays in the windows of department stores like Lord & Taylor. As he seemed reasonably well-spoken (from which I assumed he was reasonably intelligent), we accepted him as a jury member, as did defendants' counsel, without further questioning. After the trial, the juror approached me and said that he had found the engineering aspects of the case particularly interesting because he was a PhD candidate in engineering at Columbia! Had that fact been elicited in the *voir dire*, I believe it highly likely that he would have been stricken from the jury—at least by the insurance company defendants.

I remember being surprised that the defendants' trial counsel, Arthur Brook, who was a partner in a small insurance defense firm, was so effective as a trial lawyer. He had an enviable rapport with the jury. I wondered how he had developed his trial skills. The answer, I learned from him after the trial, was that he had for many years been a lawyer in the Criminal Defense Division of The Legal Aid Society.

Why have I chosen to discuss this case among the many on which I have worked, apart from its unique fact pattern? The answer is that the Second Circuit's reasoning and ruling on the one occurrence–two occurrence issue established an important precedent that was applied decades later in the litigation against insurers arising out of the World Trade Center terrorist attack, where two planes flew into the twin towers as part of what was found to be a single concerted attack.

Jantzen–Burlington Coat Factory Warehouse v. Belk Brothers

In June 1982 Bill Piel received a letter from Franklin Mize, the general counsel of Jantzen, Inc., the sports apparel manufacturer, which had just been sued in the Southern District of New York, along with several other apparel manufacturers, by Burlington Coat Factory Warehouse. Many years earlier, the two had both worked as lawyers on the polio vaccine antitrust case. Mize knew that Bill Piel had retired, but expressed the hope that Bill would pass on the case "to the people who can give me the help that I am going to need in this case." Our associate Bill Farris and I turned out to be those "people."

The claim as pleaded was fairly straightforward. Belk Brothers, a large well-established retail chain in the southeastern United States, bought merchandise from manufacturers like Jantzen and typically resold it to the public at a 50 percent "keystone" markup. Burlington, which described itself in a filing with the Securities and Exchange Commission as "a chain of 31 off-price apparel stores," sold at a 25 percent markup, thereby undercutting Belk's prices.

Burlington purchased products from Jantzen surreptitiously through a dummy corporation called "Sharon Sez." Jantzen, which described its business in its annual report as selling to "department and specialty stores," thought that Sharon Sez was a specialty store in Charlotte, North Carolina, when in fact it was simply a front for Burlington. Jantzen was eventually told by Belk that the latter's representatives had found Jantzen merchandise in Burlington stores and that if Jantzen continued to sell to Burlington, Belk would cease to buy from Jantzen. Upon discovering that its nominal customer was in fact a front for a discount chain, Jantzen stopped selling to Sharon Sez.

Burlington had a store in Charlotte near one owned by Belk Brothers, and when Jantzen stopped selling to Burlington's "front," Burlington sued alleging a price-fixing conspiracy between Jantzen and Belk. Other apparel manufacturers were named as defendants based on similar allegations.

The case presented challenges for us. One of the plaintiff's principal witnesses was a former Jantzen employee who had been fired for violating a company policy. Our task was to discredit him as a witness, and in the end I believe we succeeded. An additional challenge was presented by one of our witnesses, a senior Jantzen official, who managed to appear to be lying when he was in fact telling the truth. I must confess that I was unprepared for his demeanor on the stand.

After considerable discovery, the case went to trial before Judge Leonard Sand, one of the most respected judges on the Southern District of New York bench in the past half-century. All the manufacturing defendants other than Jantzen had settled, leaving Belk and Jantzen as the sole remaining defendants at trial.

Shortly before trial Judge Sand called us in for a conference. He informed us that an ABA task force was conducting a study of jury comprehension and had invited him (and implicitly us) to participate. He proposed to convene a jury twice the normal size. He would tell them at the outset that half of them would actually decide the case, while the other half would be part of a jury study, but he would not tell the individual panel members into which group they respectively fell. With some misgivings, I agreed to Judge Sand's proposal.

And so it was that after summations and Judge Sand's charge to the jury, he stated: "The first six jurors will constitute one of the juries. You will be using this jury room.... Miss Shepard and the five jurors sitting in the second row are going to constitute a jury panel and may go to [room] 506…."

Both juries were given a special verdict form. The first question was whether Jantzen and Belk had entered into an agreement to fix or control retail prices. If they answered that question "no," the case was over. If they entered "yes," there were further questions as to whether Jantzen had terminated Burlington pursuant to that agreement, whether Burlington had been injured as a result, and, if so, what damages Burlington should receive.

Both juries retired to deliberate at 3:15 p.m. on September 25, 1986. The deliberations of the "survey jury" were videotaped. Those jurors did not notice the camera high in the corner for a few minutes. When they spied it, they quickly realized that they were part of the study to which Judge Sand had referred, but to my surprise they resumed deliberations and proceeded as though the fate of the parties was in fact in their hands. I know this because I was given a tape of their deliberations, which I watched with fascination.

At 5 p.m. the two juries asked the Court for permission to adjourn for the day. Judge Sand unhesitatingly acceded to their wish. They resumed at 10 a.m. the following morning, and not long thereafter the "real" jury announced that they had reached a verdict. They answered "no" to the first question, namely, whether the defendants had agreed to fix or control prices, and proceeded to enter a verdict for the defendants. The survey jury, in contrast, continued to deliberate for an additional two to three hours, at which point Judge Sand excused them after they reported that they were split 4–2 for the plaintiff and doubted they would be able to reach a unanimous verdict.

Think for a moment: two six-member panels drawn from the same community, having been culled in a single voir dire, having heard the same evidence and received the same instructions, reached virtually opposite decisions. The Jantzen case was a cautionary tale on the unpredictability of juries.

One final note about the case. About a week after the trial, I was walking on West 69th Street near my apartment when a car pulled over next to me, the right front window was lowered, and the driver hailed me. She told me that she had served on the jury in the Jantzen case, and I remembered her well because it became evident during the voir dire that she was bright and articulate. When answering the jury questionnaire, she described herself as a "homemaker," which masked her attentiveness and acuity. We discussed the case for a few minutes, and then she drove off. Although I cannot recall the details of our conversation three decades later, it was clear that she had a firm grasp of the evidence and Judge Sand's instructions.

20

PROCTER & GAMBLE V. BANKERS TRUST

Occasionally, but not often, after a complaint has been filed and litigation is underway, events will occur that radically change the direction and influence the outcome of the litigation. In none of my cases has this phenomenon occurred more dramatically than in the litigation I am about to describe.

* * *

In August 1994 Procter & Gamble filed a complaint against Bankers Trust Company and a wholly owned subsidiary, BT Securities Corporation, in the U.S. District Court for the Southern District of Ohio, alleging that the defendants had fraudulently induced Procter & Gamble to enter into two complex leveraged derivatives transactions known as interest-rate swaps. (A "swap" is a transaction used to hedge against risk, such as the risk of interest rate changes, or to speculate.) Procter & Gamble sought rescission of the swaps transactions, under which Procter & Gamble then owed Bankers Trust more than $100 million due to sharp interest rate increases in early 1994. Chief Judge Carl Rubin assigned the case to himself.

Procter & Gamble was headquartered in Cincinnati and was at the time, I believe, the largest private employer in the city. Procter & Gamble retained as trial counsel both its principal outside firm, Dinsmore & Shohl, and also Stanley Chesley, who had burst on the legal scene as a plaintiff's lawyer after recovering tens of millions of dollars for the families of victims in a notorious supper club fire. Our co-counsel for Bankers Trust, Tom Ridgely and Dan Buckley at Vorys,

Sater, Seymour & Pease, suspected, as did I, that Chesley had been retained because he was, in the quaint phrase, "well and favorably known" to Judge Rubin.

Not long after Procter & Gamble filed its complaint, the Securities and Exchange Commission and the Commodity Futures Trading Commission imposed a $10 million fine on BT Securities for its conduct in entering into derivatives transactions with another client. Bankers Trust separately entered into a Written Agreement with the Federal Reserve Board requiring changes in Bankers Trust's leveraged derivatives business.

Procter & Gamble sought discovery of materials relating to those matters and, when Bankers Trust refused to produce the documents invoking a regulation promulgated by the Federal Reserve Board, Procter & Gamble filed a motion to compel production. Judge Rubin granted the motion in a telephone conference, at the outset of which he made his views crystal clear (quoting from the transcript): "I have great respect for the Federal Reserve…but…I don't give a damn what their regulations are." Judge Rubin continued, addressing us as Bankers Trust's counsel: "I don't believe the Federal Reserve can do anything to you…. If they do, I will enjoin them. If necessary, I'll hold them in contempt." Judge Rubin also rejected our attempted invocation of the bank examination privilege, holding that the privilege, which was widely accepted in the financial services community, "doesn't exist." In short, he granted Procter & Gamble's motion.

We filed a petition for a writ of mandamus (an order to a lower court, in this context an order for appellate review) in the Court of Appeals for the Sixth Circuit to vacate Judge Rubin's order. The Federal Reserve Board and the New York Clearing House filed amicus curiae ("friend of the court") briefs supporting our petition. The Court of Appeals held that as a general matter the Federal Rules of Civil Procedure trumped Federal Reserve regulations prohibiting disclosure, but remanded with directions to Judge Rubin to consider the Federal Reserve's assertion of a bank examination privilege as to any deliberative (that is, non-factual) material.

The Court of Appeals then granted our motion, joined in by the Federal Reserve Board, to stay its mandate to permit us to file a certiorari petition in the United States Supreme Court. When that petition was denied, Bankers Trust proceeded to produce to Procter & Gamble approximately 5,500 tape recordings, including recordings of internal conversations, and 300,000 pages of other materials.

After reviewing the produced materials, Procter & Gamble filed a motion to amend its complaint to add, among others, RICO claims under Title IX of the Organized Crime Control Act of 1970 ("RICO" is an acronym for "racketeer influenced and corrupt organizations"). By that time, Judge Rubin had died, and Chief Judge Gilbert Merritt of the Sixth Circuit, which included Ohio, Michigan, and other states, assigned the case not to one of the other judges of the Southern District of Ohio, as would be the normal course, but rather to John Feikens, the Chief Judge of the Eastern District of Michigan, who normally held court in Detroit. Chief Judge Merritt gave no explanation for that selection, and one can only speculate whether the fact that Cincinnati, the principal seat of the Southern District of Ohio, was Procter & Gamble's "home town" entered into his thinking.

Judge Feikens granted the motion to add a RICO claim, rejecting our argument that Procter & Gamble had been dilatory and holding that our contentions as to the sufficiency of the proposed pleading could be made in a motion to dismiss after the pleading had been filed.

In due course we made a motion to dismiss six counts

of the amended complaint and for summary judgment as to three other counts. Judge Feikens granted the motion in a lengthy opinion. He concluded that the swap agreements were not "securities" under either the federal securities laws or the Ohio counterpart and that the agreements were exempt from the Commodity Exchange Act. Judge Feikens also rejected Procter & Gamble's fiduciary duty and negligent misrepresentation claims because "BT and P&G are sophisticated corporations whose dealings were on a business level." However, he sustained the fraud claim and pointedly stated that his "rulings should not be misinterpreted.... plaintiff's case will proceed to trial."

The day following the decision, after changes in interest rates had greatly reduced the amount in dispute, the parties signed a settlement agreement and a stipulation dismissing the action.

* * *

The Procter & Gamble suit against Bankers Trust has been and will continue to be etched indelibly in my memory for a reason wholly unrelated to its merits.

Early in the case Judge Rubin had entered, with the consent of both parties, a protective order sealing the complaint and other papers to be filed. Thus, Procter & Gamble's motion to amend was filed under seal, as were the proposed pleading annexed to the motion and the RICO case statement detailing the factual basis for that claim.

On September 13, 1995, I received out of the blue a call from Linda Himelstein, who identified herself as a *Business Week* reporter. She invited me to comment, as Bankers Trust's counsel, on the proposed amended complaint. I told her that I could not and would not do so because the pleading was under seal and the subject of a protective order. I urged her to consult with *Business Week*'s legal advisers before disclosing the contents of sealed court papers.

I promptly called Tom Ridgley, who informed Procter & Gamble's counsel, and the two of them tried to call Judge Feikens. He had left for the day, but his secretary offered to call him and, if he so wished, to arrange a conference call with counsel. While I was awaiting that call, my partner Rich Klapper, who was working with me on the case, entered my office. He informed me that *Business Week* was published by the McGraw-Hill Companies, which was a client of our firm. I had not previously known of the *Business Week*–McGraw Hill connection or the client relationship.

I anticipated the conference call with Judge Feikens at any moment and did not know how to forestall it. When the call came shortly thereafter, I identified myself, but did not thereafter participate in the conversation because of the client conflict of which I had moments earlier learned. On being told that *Business Week* had a copy of a pleading that had been filed under seal, Judge Feikens immediately decided to issue an order prohibiting publication of the pleading's contents pending a hearing, which he proceeded to schedule.

A few days later, I flew to San Antonio to attend the annual meeting of the American College of Trial Lawyers. While at the American Airlines Admirals Club in the Dallas airport on Friday awaiting my connecting flight, I received a message to call my office. When I did so, I was stunned to learn that Linda Himelstein had received a copy of the Procter & Gamble motion papers from a lawyer in our firm. That lawyer had not known that the papers had been sealed and had thought that providing a copy of the filed complaint was a simple accommodation to a reporter with whom the lawyer was acquainted.

While I was in San Antonio, I spent almost the entire

weekend on the phone trying to learn what had happened and discussing the impact on Bankers Trust and McGraw-Hill, our relationships with both clients, and the potential public embarrassment to our firm. In my very first appearance before Judge Feikens a few days later, I felt obliged to apologize to him in front of the assembled lawyers for our firm's unknowing participation in a clear violation of a protective order. Judge Feikens could have chastised our firm, but he did not. Instead, he accepted my apology and proceeded to address the issues.

Judge Feikens heard McGraw-Hill's request to vacate the temporary restraining order on September 27. No one from Sullivan & Cromwell attended that hearing because of the Bankers Trust/McGraw-Hill client conflict. Judge Feikens scheduled a hearing two days later on Proctor & Gamble's motion to amend. I decided that I could ethically argue for Bankers Trust in opposition to the latter motion, which was unrelated in my mind to the question whether the sealing order should be lifted and *Business Week* left free to publish what it had learned from the sealed court papers. However, at the outset of the September 29 hearing Judge Feikens announced that he considered the issues regarding the protective order and the motion to amend to be "closely related." As the argument progressed, I realized that I was approaching perilously close to the line of what I could properly argue, and I turned the argument over to Tom Ridgley—without, I should add, advocating any position on behalf of Bankers Trust that was contrary to the position being advocated by McGraw-Hill that it was free to publish the court papers in its possession.

On October 3, 1995, Judge Feikens issued two opinions, one denying McGraw-Hill's request to lift the restraining order and the other granting the motion to amend. In the former opinion, he stated:

> [W]hile I am here holding that *Business Week* cannot publish the information it obtained illegally and in violation of protective order, this same information has become a part of the public record and may be disseminated by anyone so interested.

The Court of Appeals for the Sixth Circuit vacated the temporary restraining order, which Judge Feikens had transformed into a permanent injunction. With Judge Brown dissenting, Chief Judge Merritt, joined by Judge Martin, held that the injunction against publication was not moot, because it fell within the exception to mootness for restraints on speech that are "capable of repetition, yet evading review," citing a 1911 decision by the United States Supreme Court. On the merits, the Court of Appeals found no "compelling circumstances" warranting an injunction against publication by *Business Week*. In his opinion, Chief Judge Merritt, after describing the proceedings below, wryly observed: "This is our first experience with such a strange combination of orders." Judge Martin, concurring, was more blunt: "[T]his appeal is the culmination of a series of missteps at every stage of the case."

It is, I suppose, normal that I should wish to end the discussion of the Bankers Trust case on a positive note. Notwithstanding the unfortunate circumstances of our first encounter, Judge Feikens and I gradually formed a friendship. A year or two after the case ended, he had occasion to come to New York City, both to visit an elderly sister in New Jersey and to help the Southern District of New York dispose of its large caseload by taking cases "ready" for trial. He called me to say he would be in town, and we had a very enjoyable lunch. A few years later, when as president of the American College of Trial Lawyers I attended a dinner of the Michigan Fellows of the College, to which Judge Feikens had been elected a Fellow before ascending the bench, he was present, and we had a last opportunity to visit.

In conclusion, Judge Feikens did not shrink from conflict (or anything else to the best of my knowledge). He may not have been among the most scholarly of judges, but he presided over our case with a firm and steady hand, even when it posed extraordinary challenges that could not be anticipated. I have warm and respectful memories of Judge Feikens.

21

SOUTH CAROLINA V. UNITED STATES

In the 2008 general election, black voters turned out in large numbers that helped to elect Barack Obama President. In South Carolina for the first time in history the black voter turnout was greater than the turnout of white voters, and although President Obama did not carry the state, the usual double-digit Republican majority was reduced to a single digit. That phenomenon did not go unnoticed by the South Carolina Legislature, both houses of which were controlled by the Republican party.

For decades voters had had the option to present at the polls one of four forms of identification: (1) a state-issued voter registration card that did not have a photo, (2) a DMV-issued driver's license, (3) a passport, or (4) a military ID.

Legislation was introduced to eliminate the voter registration card and driver's license and to substitute a photo ID registration card issued only at county election offices or, alternatively, a photo ID card (but not a driver's license) issued by the State Department of Motor Vehicles.

The proposed legislation was very contentious. Black members of the South Carolina House of Representatives walked out en masse in protest for the first time in several decades. Nevertheless in May 2011 the legislation, Act R54 passed both Houses and was signed by Governor Haley. South Carolina then submitted the legislation to the U.S. Department of Justice for preclearance under the Voting Rights Act of 1965. Section 5 of the Act imposed on certain states and state subdivisions the burden of proving that any change in voting laws "neither has the purpose nor will have the effect of denying or abridging the right to vote on account of race or color." Section 4 of the Act identified the states and state subdivisions subject to Section 5 (referred to as "covered jurisdictions"). One of those jurisdictions was the State of South Carolina.[8]

Section 5 of the Voting Rights Act provided that a state whose legislation was denied preclearance by the Department of Justice could sue in federal court to overturn that determination. Venue for the suit was laid in the District of Columbia, and the case was to be heard by a three-judge court, consisting of one Court of Appeals judge and two District Court judges. On December 23, 2011, the Department of Justice, which had raised several questions after receiving South Carolina's initial submission, denied preclearance to the State's photo ID requirement, viewing it as having a disproportionate effect on minority (predominantly black) voters. South Carolina sued to overturn that determination.

Although South Carolina clearly desired to have the photo ID requirement reinstated in time for it to be in effect for the November 2012 general election, the State delayed filing its complaint until February 8, 2012, almost seven weeks after the Justice Department denial of preclearance, even though that determination cannot have come as a surprise. To compound that delay, South Carolina did not accompany the

---

[8] The Voting Rights Act had been enacted originally in 1965 after lengthy hearings that revealed voting practices in many states that had had a disproportionate impact on black voters. The statute was reenacted five times, most recently in 2006, again after extensive hearings that satisfied Congress that its provisions were still needed. In June 2013, the United States Supreme Court in *Shelby County, Alabama v. Holder* held Section 4 of the Act unconstitutional, freeing all states and state subdivisions theretofore subject to Section 5 from its restrictions. Section 5 itself remained in effect, but there were no state entities subject to its provisions; it was a toothless tiger. I cannot commend too highly Justice Ginsburg's dissenting opinion in *Shelby County.* Its reasoning is irrefutable (at least to me), and the prose is as inexorable as an ocean tide.

complaint with a request for expedited treatment, which at the time seemed to me incomprehensible and inexcusable. In retrospect, however, that delay may have been calculated, that is, based on a belief that the Court, in order to permit its decision to take effect for the November 2012 election, would impose a crushingly compressed schedule for pretrial proceedings. That is in fact what the Court did. But I should not get ahead of myself.

Sullivan & Cromwell became involved in response to a request for assistance sent by the Lawyers' Committee for Civil Rights Under Law (the "Lawyers' Committee") to law firms that had previously expressed an interest in helping it. I have had a long association with the Lawyers' Committee (which I will describe later), and my partner Garrard ("Garry") Beeney volunteered to lead a team to represent the Lawyers' Committee in the suit. The team included associates Peter Steciuk, Taly Dvorkis, Ted McCombs, Sean Camoni, and Alicia Amdur. Mark Posner of the Lawyers' Committee legal staff, a veritable encyclopedia of learning on Voting Rights Act law, worked closely with our team. I did not have a speaking role in court, but participated in all the strategizing and decision-making, sat at counsel's table, and joined in writing and editing all written submissions to the Court. In trial lawyer parlance, I was "second chair."

The Lawyers' Committee was not the only intervenor. The ACLU, the Brennan Center for Justice at NYU Law School, the South Carolina state conference of the NAACP, the NAACP Legal Defense Fund, the South Carolina League of Women Voters, and four South Carolina citizens also intervened. As the litigation progressed, Garry Beeney's leadership gradually came to be implicitly recognized by other intervenor counsel, and he assumed the role of principal advocate for all of the intervenors.

The statutorily prescribed three-judge panel consisted of Circuit Court Judge Brett M. Kavanaugh and District Court Judges John Bates and Cathleen Kollar-Kotelly. Judge Kavanaugh, who presided, had earned his spurs as a member of Independent Counsel Kenneth Starr's staff and then as Associate Counsel to President George W. Bush. Judge Kavanaugh was a member of the Federalist Society and was reputed to hold conservative views on many issues. I do not believe he had had experience with the Voting Rights Act of 1965; at least he was silent during the first days of trial, though, as we shall see, he played a prominent role in its last stages. I assumed—wrongly as it turned out—that our arguments would not resonate with Judge Kavanaugh.

Judge John D. Bates had been a District Judge since 2001. From 1980 to 1997 he had been an Assistant United States Attorney in the District of Columbia, including service as Deputy Independent Counsel to the Whitewater Investigation. Judge Bates was crisp and to the point in his comments and questions from the bench. He was not shy about expressing his views, and when he did so, his meaning was never in doubt. Most significantly, Judge Bates was intimately familiar with voting rights issues; he had presided as trial judge over the *Shelby County* case and had ruled against the State.

The final member of the panel and senior in service as a judge, Colleen Kollar-Kotelly, had been appointed by President Clinton in 1997 while serving as a judge of the Criminal Division of the District of Columbia Superior Court. Like Judge Bates, Judge Kollar-Kotelly had had recent experience with the Voting Rights Act, having served as a member of the three-judge panel in *United States v. Florida*, which was decided in plaintiff's favor in August 2012 only two weeks before the trial in the South Carolina action.

The initial pretrial conference in our case was held on

April 13, 2012. On April 26, the Court entered a Scheduling and Procedures Order, prescribing in minute detail the sequence of procedural steps to be taken by the parties culminating in a three-day trial at the end of July and beginning of August to be followed by a decision in "early September." Judge Bates issued a "concurring statement," in which Judge Kollar-Kotelly joined, expressing "concerns" about South Carolina's nonchalant approach in a case in which the State avowedly wanted a decision that could be implemented for the November 2012 election.

At the Court's request for the latest date the new photo ID requirement could be implemented before the election, Marci Andino, Chair of the State Election Commission, submitted an affidavit giving August 1, 2012, as that date. Yet at the following pretrial hearing, the State's counsel asked that the Court decide the case by September 7 without explaining why the Andino affidavit submitted one month earlier had been in error.

Judge Bates observed at that hearing that "nearly all of the relevant information is in South Carolina's possession," which necessarily meant that the compressed schedule prescribed by the Court would impose greater burdens on the United States and the intervenor-defendants than on the State in evaluating the large number of documents expected to be produced by the State.

In the ensuing weeks, South Carolina continued to produce materials responsive to the defendant's and intervenor-defendants' document requests, necessitating not one but two revisions of the scheduling order. I am not accusing the State of deliberately dilatory conduct. Let's just say that when it came to providing information, State officials did not demonstrate the sense of urgency that might have been expected of a litigant desiring an early decision. They also did not appear to be well organized.

Depositions of fact witnesses and experts proceeded on multiple tracks, and both sides served requests to admit and requests to take judicial notice. On August 7, the Court issued a "Trial Procedures Order" and then on August 13 a "Clarification" of that Order, prescribing in minute detail the procedures to be followed before and at trial.

Finally, the trial commenced on Monday, August 27. The panel allowed a total of twenty-eight hours for trial over four days, seven hours a day, which seemed to me then and now overly compressed for a case of such complexity and significance, but which in the end surprisingly proved adequate. Each side was allotted fourteen hours, and on the defense side the Panel gave the Department of Justice nine hours and the intervenors collectively five hours.

The two principal issues were whether South Carolina Act R54 had been enacted with a discriminatory purpose and whether it would have a disproportionately adverse effect on black voters. On the first issue, several prominent legislators and the Lieutenant Governor testified. Although I was fully satisfied that a discriminatory purpose could be inferred from the totality of the evidence, I also believed that the panel would be very reluctant to attribute a discriminatory purpose to a sovereign state. Indeed, Judge Kavanaugh specifically referred at one point to the doctrine of "constitutional avoidance," that is, the search for an interpretation of a state statute "in a way to avoid a conflict with federal law."

As for the discriminatory effects part of the case, I believe we successfully showed that blacks would have a more difficult time than whites traveling to the county election office or DMV to obtain the new photo ID. We introduced evidence that relatively fewer blacks than whites owned cars, as well as evidence of the absence of any or at least adequate public transportation in most counties. To drive home the latter point, we had one witness demonstrate, using a map created for the purpose as a visual aid, that it would take a citizen living in the far northeastern reaches of Charleston County more than ten hours and two or three transfers to make the round trip to the country election office or DMV to obtain the required photo ID. I had worked with the expert for several hours to create a map that would have a strong visual impact on the viewer.

Ultimately, the defensibility of the photo ID requirement would turn on the interpretation placed on a statutory exception to that requirement for a would-be voter who had a "reasonable impediment" that prevented him or her from obtaining one of the prescribed forms of photo ID. I may be accused of being unduly cynical—though in this instance I don't believe I am—but to me the political genius of that exception was that it would be administered by local polling officials, who were overwhelmingly Republican and had a long history of discriminatory behavior.

If there had been any question as to how closely the panel members were paying attention and the seriousness with which they took their responsibility, it was dispelled in an extraordinary interplay just before the luncheon recess on Thursday, the fourth day of trial.

First, Judge Bates asked whether the State would have sufficient time to implement the statute for the November general election if a decision were rendered no later than October 1. Then Judge Kavanaugh asked how the "reasonable impediment" exception would be applied. Judge Bates "add[ed] one more" question, namely, who had the authority to interpret that statutory language: the State Election Commission; its Executive Director, Marci Andino, who was a central witness at the trial; the county election commissioners; or the Attorney General.

Judge Kavanaugh then asked for South Carolina's view regarding the requirement that an affidavit proffering a "reasonable impediment" be notarized. What proof of identity would the notary require? Judge Bates asked that South Carolina answer the foregoing questions by the end of the following day.

I found, and continue to find, that brief interplay among the judges to be an extraordinary revelation of their individual and collective mental processes as they worked through the difficult issues of great importance confronting them. I cannot recall being present during a similar opening of the curtain into the judicial decision-making process.

Before the Court recessed on Friday at the end of the trial, South Carolina Attorney General Alan Wilson requested and was given leave to address the Court. He summarized the responses to the Panel's questions which the State would elaborate in a written submission to be filed later that day. Those responses, when filed, included an extraordinary invitation to the Court to interpret the "reasonable impediment" provision in whatever way the Court deemed necessary to sustain the photo ID requirement. To be precise, the State represented that "[i]f the Court believes any interpretation or implementation procedures would be necessary for preclearance, the State welcomes such guidance and will implement Act R54 accordingly." As we shall see, the Court's decision provided that guidance in unmistakable terms.

One week after the trial all parties submitted detailed Proposed Findings of Fact and Conclusions of Law, then Responses to the opposing side's proposals, and finally on September 17 Replies to the Responses. The record was then closed.

Before turning to the Court's decision, I want to describe the conditions under which we endeavored to shoulder the enormous burdens which the trial thrust on us. At Garry Beeney's suggestion, we turned a conference room in Sullivan & Cromwell's Washington, D.C., office into a war room. Each of our associates had a desktop and work space around the long conference room table, so that we could instantly confer as questions arose deserving of the collective views of the group. Virtually all of our waking hours not in the courtroom were spent toiling away in the war room or the individual offices Garry and I had been assigned. I do not exaggerate when I say that the level of effort and collaboration required was unprecedented in my experience. I felt and continued to feel great pride in the collective labors of my colleagues, who were brilliantly led by Garry Beeney.[9]

On October 10, 2012, the Court issued its decision in the form of an opinion by Judge Kavanaugh and separate concurring opinions by Judges Bates and Kollar-Kotelly. While the Panel upheld the constitutionality of the photo ID requirement, Judge Kavanaugh left no doubt as to the Panel's interpretation of the "reasonable impediment" provision. A voter seeking to invoke that exception to the photo ID requirement would be required to present some form of identification and complete an affidavit stating the voter's reason for not obtaining a photo ID.

> So long as the voter does not lie about his or her identity or the reason he or she has not obtained a photo ID, the reason that the voter gives must be accepted by

---

[9] I am not alone in admiring Garry Beeney's performance in this case. The Department of Justice trial team ceded two of its precious nine hours of allotted trial time to the intervenor-defendants when it appeared we were about to exhaust our allotted five hours. And Tom Perez, then the Assistant Attorney General in charge of the Civil Rights Division, after sitting in on the trial one day, sent Garry a personal note saying that he (Perez) had wondered, after listening to Garry in court, who that "terrific" civil rights lawyer was.

> the county board and the ballot must be counted.... [S]tate and county officials may *not* review the reasonableness of the voter's explanation (and, furthermore, may review the explanation for falsity only if someone challenges the ballot) (emphasis in the original).

Judge Kavanaugh's opinion went on to give illustrations of the reasons a voter might give for not having one of the prescribed photo IDs: work, looking for work, lack of a car to drive to the county election office, lack of money to take public transportation, child care, and others. "[T]he county board [of elections] may not second-guess the *reasonableness* of the asserted reason, only its *truthfulness"* (emphasis in the original).

Judge Kavanaugh also warned the State against any narrowing of, or variance from, the Court's interpretation of the "reasonable impediment" exception. "We have no doubt that the appropriate federal court would entertain complaints and issue appropriate injunctions if South Carolina were to narrow the interpretation of the reasonable impediment provision articulated here without first obtaining the required pre-clearance of any such change."

Judge Bates introduced his brief concurring opinion with the pithy observation: "First, to state the obvious, Act R54 as now precleared is not the R54 enacted in May 2011." He continued: "An evolutionary process has produced a law that accomplishes South Carolina's important objectives while protecting every individual's right to vote...."

I do not exaggerate when I say that the "evolution" of this case (to borrow Judge Bates' apt description) was unprecedented in my experience. Although Judge Kavanaugh remained silent in the first days of the trial while his colleagues, Judges Bates and Kollar-Kotelly, peppered both sides with questions without giving any indication of their leanings, Judge Kavanaugh came to the fore on the final trial day, and the two District Court judges subtly acknowledged his leadership of the panel. All three were understandably hesitant to strike down a state law as unconstitutional. So they effectively rewrote the law, as Judge Bates stated.

I have been in no other litigation where, as here, it can truly be said that we "lost the battle, but won the war."

* * *

Throughout the case, I wondered who had masterminded the spate of voter photo ID bills enacted after President Obama's 2008 election. Within a month after the Court's decision in the South Carolina case, I found the answer in a *New Yorker* profile by Jane Mayer of Hans von Spakovsky, a Republican lawyer who served in the administration of George W. Bush, Jr., and thereafter became a senior legal fellow at the Heritage Foundation, a well-known conservative think tank. Von Spakovsky spoke and wrote widely about the growing, widespread phenomenon of voter fraud and the need for a photo ID requirement as a prerequisite to voting. Von Spakovsky found a receptive ear in the American Legislative Exchange Council (ALEC), which sent proposed legislative language incorporating the photo ID requirement to conservative legislators in various states. South Carolina was undoubtedly one of those states.

When interviewed by Jane Mayer for the profile, Von Spakovsky identified as an expert who would confirm the widespread peril of voter-impersonation fraud Robert Pastor at American University. Yet when Mayer called him, far from backing up von Spakovsky's dire warnings, Pastor said: "I don't think that voter impersonation fraud is a serious problem." Perhaps Congressman John Lewis, the legendary civil rights leader and legislator, summed up Von Spakovsky's crusade best: "He's trying to create a cure where there is no sickness."

In fact, there was *no* evidence at the trial of our case of a single instance of voter impersonation fraud!

One final observation: Of all the cases I have worked on over a half-century, the South Carolina voting rights litigation was the most satisfying for what we accomplished, for the intensity of the effort required and expended, and for a rare insight into the judicial decision-making process at work.

22

DERIVATIVE LITIGATION

A large law firm such as Sullivan & Cromwell with many sizable corporate clients in diverse sectors of the economy is called upon with some frequency to defend so-called "derivative" suits, that is, actions brought by shareholders derivatively on behalf of a corporation against its officers, directors, and occasionally third parties, in which the plaintiff alleges either that the directors and officers have wrongfully refused a shareholder demand to bring suit for conduct injuring the corporation or, alternatively, that such a demand is excused because imposing it would require the directors and officers to sue themselves.

I have been involved in a number of derivative litigations dating back to the '60s, including one that afforded me an opportunity to argue in the Supreme Court of Delaware. The three most recent such litigations described below (I refer to them as "litigations" rather than individual "cases" because after one derivative complaint is filed, copycat complaints normally follow) are unique in my experience because while they involved three separate large corporations, there was overlapping membership on the three boards of directors, and I believe that the second representation came to Sullivan & Cromwell on the recommendation of directors in the first and that the third resulted from a recommendation of the directors in the second. I will discuss them sequentially.

NYNEX

On January 9, 1990, the *Wall Street Journal* reported that an audit performed by the Common Carrier Bureau of the Federal Communications Commission had concluded that

NYNEX had overcharged its wholly-owned operating subsidiaries, New York Telephone Co. and New England Telephone & Telegraph Co., in their procurement of goods and services from a third NYNEX subsidiary, NYNEX Materiel Enterprises Co. ("MECO"). Several of the assertions in the *Journal* article were incorporated in a derivative complaint filed the very same day in the Supreme Court in Manhattan. I remember being astonished at the speed with which the plaintiff's lawyers had moved and wondered at what hour they had first seen the *Journal.* The following day the NYNEX Board received a demand letter from the lawyers for another shareholder, and other demand letters followed.

Two quite distinct charges were woven together in the demand letters and complaints: (1) a charge that, independently of regulatory prohibitions, NYNEX had compelled its two telephone operating companies to purchase goods and services from MECO and other NYNEX subsidiaries that could have been procured more cheaply from unaffiliated suppliers, and (2) a charge that, whether or not New York Telephone and New England Telephone could have obtained goods and services more cheaply elsewhere, the profit realized by MECO on those sales exceeded allowable regulatory limits.

In February 1990, the NYNEX Board, advised by the Davis Polk firm, created a Special Review Committee consisting of all nine board members who were not present or former NYNEX officers. The authorizing board resolution empowered the committee to investigate the matters raised in the complaint and demand letters, as well as any related matters. The committee was empowered to "exercise the powers of the Board of Directors" regarding those matters.

I am not certain who at our firm was first approached by the Special Committee, but I was brought into the matter by

Loeber Landau, a universally respected and liked partner in what we then called the General Practice Group. Loeber was almost certainly as knowledgeable as anyone in the firm on corporate governance issues, and that expertise was critical to our engagement. I in turn recruited one of our Litigation Group's brightest senior associates, Michael Lacovara, and a few junior associates.

We reviewed a substantial number of federal, state, consultants', and internal reports and the entire record of the recently concluded New York Public Service Commission hearings dealing with affiliated transaction issues. In addition to reviewing testimony given in other proceedings, we conducted forty-one formal interviews. A committee member attended each interview, and a compilation of interview memoranda and related documents was given to all committee members. The committee met on eleven occasions between March 1990 and April 1991 and reviewed general procurement policies and practices, as well as a large number of specific areas in which improprieties had allegedly occurred.

At the conclusion of its investigation, the committee rendered a 185-page report discussing in detail each of the allegations of misconduct that had come to its attention. There were many such allegations, and they were far-ranging: they included several different areas of procurement and unrebutted charges that MECO's Vice President-Purchasing had organized trips to Florida attended by MECO employees and representatives of companies that did business with MECO.

The committee found no evidence to suggest that the contracts between NYNEX and suppliers attending the Florida "conventions" had been disadvantageous to NYNEX. The committee further found that NYNEX and its affiliates had strengthened their commitment to compliance with external requirements and tightened internal procurement policies and procedures. Finally, the committee determined that it would not be in the best interests of NYNEX and its stockholders to continue any of the five pending derivative suits or take other remedial action beyond that already being pursued. In sum, the plaintiffs' shareholder demands were refused.

After reviewing the Special Review Committee report, plaintiffs' counsel in the Delaware Chancery Court derivative suits realized that the report was both comprehensive and impregnable and that they could not sustain their burden of showing that the refusal of their shareholder demands was wrongful, so they moved for a voluntary dismissal, coupled (surprise!) with a request for an award of attorneys' fees. They argued that their litigation efforts had been responsible for the remedial changes in NYNEX's corporate structure. The defendants countered with a motion for involuntary dismissal.

After hearing argument in August 1992, Chancellor William Allen delivered an opinion from the bench granting defendants' motion, denying plaintiffs' motion, and dismissing all of the actions with prejudice. He ruled (1) that the plaintiffs had conceded, by making a demand on the Board to bring suit, that the Board was disinterested, and (2) that the plaintiffs had not challenged either the good faith or the thoroughness of the investigation conducted by the Special Review Committee. John R. ("Jack") Stafford, chairman of the committee, called me to express the committee's pleasure at the outcome.

The Special Review Committee had reserved in its initial report one matter that had been committed to its charge: an unresolved criminal contempt proceeding charging NYNEX with a willful violation of the Modified Final Judgment (MFJ) concluding the Department of Justice's historic antitrust case against AT&T. The contempt proceeding focused on a discontinued activity by a subsidiary that had since been sold by NYNEX. That activity, DOJ contended, constituted an "information service" prohibited by the MFJ. In February 1993, Judge Harold Greene of the United States District Court for the District of Columbia, who had presided for many years over the AT&T antitrust decree, held that NYNEX had violated the decree and was guilty of criminal contempt. The Court of Appeals reversed, holding that "the Consent Decree lacked the necessary clarity and specificity to support a finding of criminal contempt."

The Special Review Committee thereupon took up the issue of whether the board of directors had been remiss in not addressing the activity in question. As counsel to the committee, we investigated the background to the contempt proceeding and advised the committee in March 1994 that they would be justified in concluding that it would not be in the best interests of NYNEX and its shareholders to pursue claims against any present or former NYNEX officer or employee based on the questioned activity. The committee accepted our advice and issued a supplemental report to that effect.

In conclusion, I want to make special note of the performance of Jack Stafford as Chair of the NYNEX Special Review Committee. Despite his demanding responsibilities as Chairman of the Board and Chief Executive Officer of American Home Products Corporation, a pharmaceutical giant, Jack Stafford devoted countless hours to his duties as a NYNEX director. When I needed to talk to Jack Stafford, he made himself available. He was a model "outside" director.

Chemical Bank

In 1990 Chemical Bank was one of the largest foreign exchange (FX) dealers in the world, engaging in both spot and forward transactions.[10] Most often Chemical acted as a market-maker, hedging its purchases and sales with offsetting trades and making its profit on the market-makers' bid/ask spread. The FX Department received high ratings from the bank's internal auditors, and the joint examinations conducted by the New York Banking Department and the Federal Reserve Bank of New York resulted in favorable comments about Chemical's FX controls and senior management's commitment to improving the bank's overall control environment.

One of the highest-ranking employees in the bank's FX Department was Victor Gomez, who had started in Sales but was moved to Trading, where he worked directly under William Arnold, one of the bank's most highly regarded traders.

Prior to 1994 Chemical did not make a market in pesos; the Mexican government discouraged Mexican banks from entering into peso forward agreements. The Mexican Central Bank changed course in late 1992, permitting a certain form of forward agreement called a "coberatura." The North American Free Trade Agreement entered into in 1993 created a demand for FX products, and in early 1994 Gomez sought and received approval to engage in peso forward/coberatura transactions, but with a requirement of prior approval for transactions exceeding $30 million.

When President-Elect Zedillo announced in October 1994 the renewal of a "social pact" that, among other things,

---

[10] "Spot transactions" were purchases or sales of currencies for settlement within two days. "Forward transactions" were agreements to purchase or sell a specified amount of a particular currency at a negotiated exchange rate on a specific date more than two days in the future.

maintained the value of the peso within a defined trading band, Gomez began a series of unauthorized trades, in effect betting the bank's money that the peso would remain strong relative to the dollar. By December 20, 1994, Gomez held open (i.e., unhedged) positions in pesos totaling $225 million, far in excess of the limit that had been set by the bank's Market Risk Management Group. That group did not detect the violation because Gomez entered fictitious hedging transactions in the bank's trading records. In addition to the unhedged peso-forward transactions, Gomez sold six unhedged coberaturas totaling $50 million to Mexican banks, obligating Chemical to purchase pesos for dollars at a fixed rate in the future.

The week of December 19, 1994, proved to be Gomez's undoing. The Mexican government devalued the peso and two days later permitted the peso to trade freely. The combination of the peso devaluation and the close of the bank's FX fiscal year caused bank officials to scrutinize Gomez's trading activities more closely, and upon learning of his unauthorized trades, the bank fired Gomez.

On January 3, 1995, Chemical publicly announced that it had suffered an estimated pre-tax loss of $70 million because of Gomez's unauthorized trades. Within a week six derivative actions were filed in New York Supreme Court. Plaintiffs' counsel agreed to consolidate the actions (as the court would in any event have ordered) and to file an amended consolidated complaint. That pleading, when filed, charged the twenty defendant directors, sixteen of whom were neither officers nor employees of Chemical, with having failed to exercise their oversight responsibilities and alleged that their failure had caused the bank's loss. None of the shareholder plaintiffs had made a pre-suit demand on the board to take appropriate remedial action, and none alleged facts that might have excused the failure to make such a demand.

At a meeting on February 21, 1995, the Chemical Board created a five-member Special Committee on Peso Litigation to make recommendations to the entire board for responding to the derivative actions. In contrast to the NYNEX matter, the special committee created by the Chemical Board was not vested with the powers of the full board. There had been a shareholder demand that suit be brought in the NYNEX matter; there had not been such a demand made by the shareholder plaintiffs in Chemical. Under governing law the entire Chemical Board was in a position to decide whether legal action should be pursued.

The Chemical Board also authorized the retention of Sullivan & Cromwell as independent counsel to the Board. Why was our firm chosen when, to the best of my knowledge, we had not previously represented Chemical? The answer, I believe, lies in the fact that two of the five members of the Chemical special committee (its Chairman, Helene Kaplan, and Jack Stafford) had been members of the NYNEX special committee. Walter Shipley, Chairman and CEO of Chemical, had also been a member of the NYNEX special committee. All three had had experience working with Sullivan & Cromwell in derivative litigation and presumably had found that experience satisfactory.

In due course we moved on the defendants' behalf to dismiss the amended complaint. Justice Emily Goodman granted the motion, reaffirming the bedrock principle of corporate governance that "the bringing of a derivative claim against corporate directors is the corporation's prerogative," unless the directors had themselves authorized or participated in wrongdoing, had ignored "obvious danger signs of employee wrongdoing," or were so beholden to others as to be incapable of exercising independent judgment As none of those circumstances was present, Justice Goodman dismissed the complaint, but granted leave to replead.

Five of the six shareholder plaintiffs folded their tent, but the sixth filed a second amended complaint, which Justice Goodman again dismissed, this time with prejudice. Her view of the remaining plaintiff's complaint was reflected in her handwritten opinion, which was less than one page long and included the statement that the plaintiff's charge of director wrongdoing "makes no sense." The Appellate Division summarily and unanimously affirmed dismissal of the twice-amended complaint.

JPMorgan Chase

The third in this related trilogy of derivative litigations—related in that two JPMorgan Chase (JPM) directors, Jack Stafford and Helene Kaplan, had been directors of both NYNEX and Chemical Bank, and a third, Bill Harrison, JPM's Chairman, had been chairman and a director of Chemical—is itself a trilogy of cases brought by a single plaintiff, Halpert Enterprises.

In the first action, Halpert alleged that the directors had breached their fiduciary duties by failing to prevent JPM from entering into allegedly fraudulent forward transactions with Enron Corporation. Judge Sidney Stein of the Southern District of New York dismissed the complaint, with leave to replead, for failure to allege with particularity, as required by Rule 23.1 of the Federal Rules of Civil Procedure, that it would have been futile to make a demand on the directors.

Halpert's amended complaint reiterated the Enron charges and added what Judge Stein described as a "laundry list" of allegations regarding six other unrelated matters. Judge Stein dismissed this pleading as well on the same ground.

Plaintiff's lawyers finally got the message and in October

2005 made a demand on the JPM Board, referring to the seven matters previously alleged and adding an eighth. Two weeks later the JPM Board adopted a resolution directing the Audit Committee of the board to conduct an investigation. The Audit Committee retained Sullivan & Cromwell, and my partner Stephanie Wheeler and I undertook the investigation. We met with the Audit Committee on three occasions, and in April 2006 that committee rendered a report concisely discussing each of the eight separate instances of alleged wrongdoing and recommending that the demand be refused. The board accepted that recommendation.

Credit plaintiff's counsel with energy if not good judgment. They filed a third amended complaint, alleging that the board investigation had been "superficial" and that the board refusal of plaintiff's demand had been ill-informed. We again moved on defendants' behalf to dismiss, and Judge Harold Baer, to whom the case had been reassigned, granted the motion, holding that plaintiff had failed to alleged specific facts calling into question the thoroughness or good faith of the investigation underlying the demand refusal. Ruling that plaintiff's counsel had adduced no facts that might overcome the pleading bar for a derivative suit, Judge Baer denied leave to amend yet a fourth time. Plaintiff appealed to the Court of Appeals for the Second Circuit, which unanimously affirmed.

* * *

My experience in the three derivative litigations discussed above affirmed my faith in the effectiveness of the governance process of American corporations for resolving derivative claims. I know that many view this process with cynicism, believing both that it reaches a predetermined result whatever the facts unearthed and that the conclusions reached by boards of directors and their special review committees are more ritual than genuinely deliberative. I can assure you that was not true from my observation. A majority of the directors on the NYNEX, Chemical, and JPMorgan Chase boards of directors, in addition to Jack Stafford, were the chief executive or other senior officers of major corporations (Lee Raymond, Chief Executive Officer of Exxon-Mobil, and Frank Bennack, Chief Executive Officer of Hearst, both JPM directors, stand out in my memory). They all had demanding responsibilities in their "day jobs." Yet it was my observation that, without exception, they took their director responsibilities very seriously and devoted all the time required to discharge those responsibilities thoroughly and conscientiously.

23

REPRESENTING AN ACCOUNTING FIRM: DELOITTE, HASKINS & SELLS

In 1969, not long after I became a partner, John Raben asked me to take charge of the defense of Haskins & Sells, a longtime client of our firm, in a lawsuit brought in federal court in Colorado by Stephens Industries. Thus began a client relationship that lasted fifteen years and took me to federal court in San Francisco, San Diego, Dallas, Miami, Cincinnati, and Denver. It was truly a pleasure to represent a professional firm whose partners wished to understand not only the advice we provided but also the reasons underlying it.

Haskins & Sells did not have an in-house general counsel at the time. That function was effectively performed by Sullivan & Cromwell, with John Raben or a junior lawyer handling transactional matters while I bore primary responsibility for litigation wherever it was brought.

My principal contact at Haskins & Sells was Harry Weyrich, a senior partner of the firm, but I dealt as well with the managing partner, initially John Queenan, then Mike Chetkovich, and finally Mike Cook. I also spoke frequently with Ken Stringer, the ultimate authority in the firm on all accounting and auditing issues, whose soft Kentucky drawl concealed a mind as acute as any non-lawyer with whom I have worked.

Stephens Industries v. Haskins & Sells

Stephens Industries had purchased a company named Rent-A-Car Companies, which went downhill after the purchase. Stephens Industries successfully sued the seller to recover the purchase price and then sued Haskins & Sells to recover both cash advances made before the purchase and amounts that Stephens Industries was required to pay as guarantor of loans previously made to Rent-A-Car Companies.

The Stephens Industries case ultimately went to trial in December 1969. We had retained as local counsel Bob Harry of the Denver firm of Davis, Graham & Stubbs, and Bob enlisted an associate named David Ebel, who took the lead for most of the trial. David was a thoughtful, highly intelligent lawyer, who had clerked for Justice Byron White on the Supreme Court and ultimately himself became a judge of the Court of Appeals for the Tenth Circuit.

The trial commenced on Monday, December 22, 1969, before Judge William Doyle, a crusty elderly judge who brooked no nonsense. I believe Judge Doyle anticipated that the trial would take only two days or three at most, so that it would conclude before Christmas, unless the jury thought more of plaintiff's case than Judge Doyle did. Unfortunately, plaintiff's counsel was woefully inefficient in presenting his client's case, making Judge Doyle so angry that he announced on Wednesday, Christmas Eve, that the not-yet-completed trial would resume on Friday, the day after Christmas. That harsh scheduling order presented a problem for plaintiff's principal representative at trial, who lived in Iowa, and for me.

I lived in Short Hills, New Jersey, and was married with three small children; Jeff was five, Sarah three, and Paul five months. I was damned if Judge Doyle was going to prevent me from watching my children open their Christmas presents. Somehow I managed to make the last flight out of Denver to one of the New York City area airports. I was the only passenger flying in first class; the rear cabin was filled with soldiers, most presumably going home on Christmas leave. (Remember, this was during the height of the Vietnam War.) The stewardess invited me to take home the remainder of the first class wine allotment that I had not consumed. I declined the offer with thanks and asked that she take the wine back to the soldiers in the rear cabin, who drank it with pleasure.

I arrived home around 1 a.m. and was violently nauseous for the remainder of the night. But I did get to watch Jeff, Sarah, and Paul open their presents. That afternoon I was on a plane back to Denver. When the trial carried over the weekend, John Crane, the young Haskins & Sells partner who had been my primary contact, took me skiing with his family on Saturday at Winter Park, a ski resort near Denver. I had been on skis only once or twice and only in the East. I shared a lift chair with John Crane's young daughter, and when we reached the top at an altitude in excess of 10,000 feet, she jumped off the lift, said "Come on, Mr. Cooper," and then disappeared from view over the edge. I don't think I had ever been as frightened, but I could not let her down (and embarrass myself), so I followed her in terror. I snowplowed down the entire slope, trying to avoid the experienced skiers racing down the mountain.

After my overnight trip home and my skiing adventure, the outcome of the trial seemed almost anticlimactic. However, the jury did render a verdict for all defendants. Judge Doyle entered judgment, and plaintiff appealed. The Court of Appeals grappled with the question whether an accounting firm was liable to someone other than its client for ordinary negligence, a question as to which there was no precedent under the governing law of Colorado. The Court of Appeals answered that question in the negative and affirmed the judgment for Haskins & Sells.

Pearson v. Ecological Science Corporation

Haskins & Sells had the misfortune of serving as independent auditors of a high-flying Miami-based entity named Ecological Science Corporation ("Ecological"). In early 1971, the Securities and Exchange Commission sued Ecological for issuing statements such as that it had developed an "economical on-site disposable black box and system that results in essentially pollutant-free discharges to the atmosphere and can capture and convert to useful energy some of the heat content of the garbage and refuse being disposed of." Need I elaborate on the corporation's puffery? Ecological and its President, Harold Koenig, consented to the issuance of a preliminary and then a permanent SEC injunction, and Ecological revised downward its 1969 per-share earnings. The stock price plummeted, and the SEC suspended over-the-counter trading in its shares.

As was predictable, complaints—sixteen in all—were filed in various districts, and we were off to the races. Although the SEC had sued and obtained injunctive relief in the Southern District of New York, the true locus of the litigation was the Southern District of Florida, and the Judicial Panel on Multidistrict Litigation ordered all of the cases filed elsewhere transferred to that district for coordinated pretrial proceedings.

A few words about the lineup of counsel and the presiding judge: Lead plaintiff's counsel was Hugo Black, Jr., son of the Supreme Court Justice and a widely known plaintiff's lawyer in the Miami area. One of the junior lawyers on the plaintiffs' side was Alan Greer, with whom I developed a close friendship over the years. Ecological was represented by Stuart Summit, a New York lawyer who had initially been an associate with a large firm but had left to form a boutique firm, Miller & Summit. Stu Summit was a very able and justifiably self-confident lawyer. One of the individual defendants was represented by Sidney Aronovitz, a thoroughly engaging solo practitioner who was later appointed to the federal court. Haskins & Sells retained as local counsel Reginald L. ("Reggie") Williams, a member of a distinguished Miami firm, who graciously deferred to me even though he was probably three decades older—and much more experienced—than I.

The case was assigned to Judge Peter Fay. Rumor had it that he owed his judicial appointment to the fact that he had taught President Nixon's daughters how to water-ski at Key Biscayne. Whether or not there was truth to the rumor, Judge Fay presided over the case with skill and patience.

Our principal task was to prevent Haskins & Sells from being lumped together with its co-defendants, Ecological and its President, Koenig. At the initial pretrial hearing, I argued that if the actions were consolidated, they should not lose their separate identity. Judge Fay graciously welcomed me to his court ("Delighted to have you with us"), but proceeded to order not only that the actions be consolidated, but also that a consolidated amended complaint be filed.

At the first hearing after that filing, on March 2, 1973, Judge Fay expressed sympathy with the plaintiffs' argument that the Court should maintain the litigation as a class action under Federal Rule of Civil Procedure 23(a) because "it would save a lot of time and a lot of money." Indeed, the Court said: "I would love to declare this a class action." Facing an uphill battle, I argued that the case involved "a plethora of misstatements, not just one or two, thereby distinguishing it from the cases which plaintiff has relied on," and that there was no "factual nexus among the alleged misrepresentations and omissions…antedating the litigation and not supplied by an allegation drafted by a lawyer that everything was done pursuant to a common course of conduct."

Judge Fay accepted my argument and denied plaintiffs' motion for class action treatment, holding that individual questions predominated over the questions of fact and law common to all members of the class, that "insurmountable obstacles…would prevent the named plaintiffs from 'fairly and adequately' representing the interests of the proposed class," and that intervention by individual claimants would be superior to class action treatment.

Plaintiffs appealed the order denying class action treatment. The defendants moved to dismiss the appeal for lack of jurisdiction on the ground that the order denying class certification was not an appealable "final" order. The Court of Appeals first entered an order summarily dismissing the appeal and then denied a motion for rehearing and rehearing en banc (that is, rehearing by all active judges on the Court), and the Supreme Court denied certiorari.

Remember that this action was filed only seven years after Rule 23 of the Federal Rules of Civil Procedure was substantially revised to describe the categories of class actions with which lawyers are familiar today. I suspect that if the allegations in this litigation had been made in a complaint filed today, the motion for class certification might have been granted.

The parties proceeded with discovery, which was relatively uneventful except for the deposition of Haskins & Sells partner Harry Weyrich. This was the first deposition I had attended that was videotaped. Harry Weyrich was a devoted pipe smoker and was dismayed when I told him that he could not smoke his pipe during the deposition because his videotaped image would be veiled in smoke, calling to mind the three witches in *Macbeth*. I did tell him, however, that he could bring his unlit pipe to the deposition.

Now, if you know an inveterate pipe smoker, you know that they like to perform all sorts of rituals with their pipes: cleaning the barrel, tapping the pipe on a hard surface, etc. Well, Harry Weyrich was no different than other inveterate pipe smokers. As this was in the early days of videotaping, the technician was surrounded by electronic equipment in a room adjacent to the one in which the deposition was being held. The voice-recording equipment was connected by through-the-wall wiring to the microphone placed in front of the witness. The deposition proceeded without interruption until Harry Weyrich pounded his pipe on the table (presumably to dislodge any remnants of tobacco), at which point the technician burst into the room and announced that the pipe-slamming had to end before his hearing was permanently damaged.

After several months of intensive discovery, the parties (by this time there were nearly 100 plaintiffs and intervenors) entered into a stipulation of settlement. A portion of the settlement proceeds were placed in escrow. The stipulation provided that if during the ensuing eighteen months one or more actions were brought against Haskins & Sells asserting claims "similar" to those being settled, Haskins & Sells had a right to rescind the settlement as to the escrowed funds. All of the plaintiffs and intervenors approved the settlement in writing. However, almost immediately two attempts were made to derail the settlement.

An Ecological shareholder who had previously not participated in the litigation filed a motion to intervene, contending that consummation of the settlement would breach duties owed to members of the class on whose behalf the litigation had been brought. Judge Fay denied the motion as untimely and because the stipulation of settlement did not affect his rights since he was free to file his own complaint.

The other attempt to derail the settlement was made by two purchasers of Ecological shares who had signed ratifications of the proposed settlement. They claimed, among other things, that the terms of the proposed settlement had been misrepresented to them by lead plaintiffs' counsel. After briefing and argument, Judge Fay rejected that claim, finding that the two plaintiffs had "knowledgably accepted" the stipulation of settlement.

Both the would-be intervenor and the recanting plaintiffs appealed to the Court of Appeals for the Fifth Circuit. To my surprise, the Securities and Exchange Commission weighed in, filing an amicus curiae brief supporting the appellants. The Court of Appeals nevertheless affirmed the District Court resoundingly in a unanimous decision. As was to be expected, the disappointed appellants sought certiorari review by the United States Supreme Court, which was denied.

Reingold v. Deloitte, Haskins & Sells

For several decades a large number of accounting firms located throughout the world, most containing some combination of the names "Deloitte" and "Haskins & Sells," practiced professional accountancy in close cooperation and coordination. To strengthen their professional relationship, an unincorporated organization known as DH&S International was established in 1976 by agreement among more than forty firms organized under the laws of different nations. The DH&S International Executive Committee granted to each of the affiliated firms the right to use the name "Deloitte, Haskins & Sells." Each affiliated firm remained solely responsible for the performance of its professional engagements, and the firms did not share profits or losses.

The trained litigator's eye can discern in this arrangement the potential for disagreement over personal jurisdiction, and that was in fact the core issue in the case I am about to describe. To complicate matters further, the financial statements in question had been audited by Yarwood, Vane & Co., whose members were, with four exceptions, identical to those of DH&S (Australia).

Representing an Australian client can pose difficulties in verbal communication across time zones. One day I had occasion to speak urgently to Rob Devenish, a partner in the Perth office of DH&S (Australia). It was about 3 p.m. in New York City and 3 a.m. in Perth. Talking to a DH&S International partner in New York, I expressed concern about trying to call Rob Devenish in Perth at that hour. Fortunately, the Perth Yacht Club was challenging the United States in the America's Cup, which was being contested that very day off Newport, Rhode Island. The partner in New York to whom I was talking told me not to worry because, he assured me, every last soul in Perth would be awake at that godforsaken hour watching the America's Cup race on television. He was proved correct when Rob picked up the phone on the second ring, fully alert.

Yarwood, Vane were the auditors for Ferrovanadium, an Australian mining company with a dismal record of continuing losses. Yarwood, Vane audited and rendered a report in Perth on the "accounts" (the Australian term for what we know as "financial statements") of Ferrovanadium for the fiscal year ended June 30, 1979. Ferrovanadium included the Yarwood, Vane report in a registration statement filed with the SEC for the issuance of American Depositary Receipts (ADRs), the equivalent of shares in a U.S. company. Ferrovanadium filed the Yarwood, Vane report on the company's accounts without that firm's consent and, indeed, contrary to the advice of Yarwood, Vane, that the Australian accounts were not sufficient for a filing with the SEC.

Ferrovanadium's losses continued, and a suit was brought on behalf of the ADR purchasers in federal court in the Southern District of New York against both DH&S and Yarwood, Vane. Notwithstanding Ferrovanadium's continuing sorry financial condition (its losses in fiscal 1979 were twice those of the preceding year) and notwithstanding Yarwood, Vane's express disclaimer as to "the fairness of the value" of Ferrovanadium's assets as recorded in the company's accounts, the plaintiffs alleged that Yarwood, Vane's report had "artificially inflated" the price of the company's ADRs. The plaintiffs were represented by Max Berger, a very able and also very amiable adversary.

We moved to dismiss as to Yarwood, Vane for lack of personal jurisdiction and for dismissal as to both that firm and DH&S for failure to state a claim. After several months, Judge Gerard Goettel issued a lengthy decision on December 6, 1984. He observed that there was "no single worldwide DH&S firm" and that the Australian firm "maintained control over its day-to-day operations" and did not share profits and losses with other DH&S firms.

Judge Goettel then parsed the various bases on which personal jurisdiction could be predicated and found all of them lacking as to the 1979 audited financial statements. He sustained the complaint to the extent it challenged the 1980 financial statements because, he found, DH&S (Australia) knew that Ferrovanadium would file its 1980 annual report, including the audited 1980 financial statements, with the SEC. Finally, Judge Goettel granted the motion to dismiss the fraud claims, but granted leave to replead those claims. Not long thereafter, the litigation was settled on terms satisfactory to DH&S (Australia) and Yarwood, Vane.

Rereading Judge Goettel's decision three decades later, I am again struck by the care and balance with which he analyzed the personal jurisdiction issues.

24

REPRESENTING LAW FIRMS

It is a high compliment for an advocate to be sought out as counsel by another lawyer or law firm. Over the years I have been privileged to represent five law firms. Two of those matters involved regulatory investigations, and a third involved a dispute between a firm and one of its partners. I do not consider it appropriate to say more about those representations. I will mention the fourth law firm representation briefly and discuss the fifth at greater length.

Chadbourne, Parke, Whiteside & Wolff

The Chadbourne firm had long represented American Tobacco Company when the "tobacco wars" erupted in the 1990s. Given the predilection of many plaintiffs' lawyers to cast their net broadly when drafting a complaint, it is not surprising that Chadbourne found itself named as a defendant in several suits brought by states seeking to recoup Medicaid payments and alleging a conspiracy to mislead the public about the hazards of smoking. Such suits were filed by, among others, Minnesota, Puerto Rico, and South Carolina. The matter was complicated by the fact that a Chadbourne partner had served in a non-legal capacity on the Board of the Center for Tobacco Research, which the plaintiffs characterized as the hub of the alleged conspiracy.

Our motion to dismiss Chadbourne for lack of personal jurisdiction was granted in the Puerto Rico action. The other actions were resolved in the global tobacco industry settlement in November 1998. Much of the credit for whatever we accomplished in this representation goes to my partner Bill Snipes and our former associate Holly Weiss.

My most pleasant memory of the matter was working with Charlie O'Neill, the Chadbourne managing partner, who quickly and fully understood the issues in the litigation and my advice for dealing with them.

O'Melveny & Myers (in re St. Johnsbury)

My representation of O'Melveny & Myers in the Chapter 11 bankruptcy proceeding of St. Johnsbury Trucking Co. is worthy of discussion principally because it is the only instance I can recall in which a judge not only committed error, but did so in a manner that disregarded, to the point of exhibiting disdain for, the rulings of a higher court. I do not voice that criticism lightly, for I have a deeply rooted respect for the judiciary, both federal and state, that antedates my becoming a lawyer. The St. Johnsbury matter is also a cautionary tale about the possible consequences of inadvertent mistakes by counsel in reviewing documents for production to an adversary in litigation.

St. Johnsbury Trucking Co. filed a Chapter 11 bankruptcy petition in June 1993 in the Southern District of New York. Bankers Trust Co. was a principal creditor of St. Johnsbury. In November 1993 St. Johnsbury (the "Debtor") and the Creditors' Committee commenced what in bankruptcy parlance is called an "adversary proceeding" in the District of Vermont against Bankers Trust. The complaint in the adversary proceeding alleged that the security interest of Bankers Trust in St. Johnsbury's receivables had not been perfected because Bankers Trust had made its Uniform Commercial Code filing in Massachusetts rather than in Vermont, where the Debtor claimed the receivables records were located. Bankers Trust had chosen Massachusetts for the filing in reliance on a written representation by William Clifford, St. Johnsbury's Chief Executive Officer, that the receivables records were in fact located in Massachusetts, not Vermont. That representation had been made in a restructuring agreement entered into a mere five months before the bankruptcy filing.

The New York Chapter 11 proceeding and the Vermont adversary proceeding were both assigned to the Honorable Francis G. Conrad, a bankruptcy judge who had been appointed in Vermont but frequently was assigned to sit in the Southern District of New York, which had a far larger bankruptcy caseload.

Bankers Trust filed a counterclaim in the Vermont adversary proceeding alleging that the Debtor and Mr. Clifford had misrepresented the location of the receivables records, which accounted for the UCC filing in Massachusetts now alleged to have been incorrect. Months later Bankers, the Debtor, and certain of the Debtor's bondholders negotiated a settlement of the Vermont adversary proceeding and agreed upon and filed a proposed Chapter 11 plan of liquidation in the New York bankruptcy proceeding.

O'Melveny & Myers, which had represented Bankers Trust in its lending relationship with St. Johnsbury, appeared for Bankers Trust in the early stages of both the bankruptcy proceeding and the adversary proceeding. However, when counsel for Clifford asserted that O'Melveny had a conflict because the mistakes described below which the firm had made in discovery had been the real cause of Bankers Trust's injury, O'Melveny promptly and properly withdrew as counsel to Bankers in the adversary proceeding and was replaced by the Winthrop, Stimson firm.

In September 1994 discovery was conducted in connection with the proposed settlement of the adversary proceeding and the Chapter 11 plan. During that discovery, O'Melveny, which continued to represent Bankers Trust in the Chapter 11 proceeding, inadvertently produced a number of privileged documents, including a memorandum by associate Adam Harris that discussed when Bankers Trust had first learned that St. Johnsbury maintained some receivables records in Vermont. Upon learning that the privileged memorandum had been produced, O'Melveny requested its return. That same day, Bankers Trust received a facsimile of a court filing by Clifford's counsel in the adversary proceeding stating that the Harris memorandum eliminated any good faith basis for Bankers Trust's counterclaim in that proceeding.

Once O'Melveny's conduct had been impugned in the adversary proceeding, the firm retained me to represent both the firm and Adam Harris in that proceeding. O'Melveny asked its partner Martin Glenn to follow the matter and liaise with me. Marty Glenn, now himself a highly respected bankruptcy judge in the Southern District of New York, was a wonderful client representative. He was as bright as they come—which you knew on meeting him even before learning that he had clerked for the legendary Henry Friendly on the Court of Appeals for the Second Circuit—and a true gentleman. I never once heard Marty Glenn raise his voice, even on occasions when I did.

Bankers Trust, which had been appearing through inside counsel, retained Robert B. Fiske, Jr. of Davis Polk, a renowned Davis Polk partner, who had been U.S. Attorney for the Southern District of New York and Independent Counsel in the Whitewater investigation. No more thoughtful, intelligent, and collaborative co-counsel could have been wished for.

At an adversary proceeding hearing on September 29, 1994, Judge Conrad stated that the Adam Harris memorandum established "a prima facie case for [Rule] 9011 sanctions" and "a prima facie case that a fraud had been perpetrated upon the Court." Judge Conrad appointed counsel for the Creditors' Committee and Clifford's counsel to conduct discovery in New York and Vermont, respectively, regarding the charge of sanctionable conduct. Not content with ordering that relief, Judge Conrad ruled that "all claims of privilege" (defined to include attorney work product) "are terminated" and ordered that documents as to which a privilege had been asserted be turned over within ten days to Clifford's counsel in the adversary proceeding.

At the ensuing hearing, Judge Conrad granted summary judgment to Clifford dismissing Bankers Trust's counterclaim in the adversary proceeding, calling it "one of the easiest summary judgments I've ever had to decide in my entire life." Judge Conrad rejected the request by Bankers Trust's counsel, Bob Fiske, for an opportunity to respond to claims first made at the hearing by Clifford's counsel. Judge Conrad similarly turned a deaf ear to my argument that under recent Second Circuit case law O'Melveny had not waived any privileges when it inadvertently produced the memorandum that had triggered Judge Conrad's rulings. I was equally unsuccessful in arguing that there was recent controlling authority that a judge could not rely on materials claimed to be privileged to make a finding of fraud and then terminate the privilege.

Judge Conrad proceeded to hold a hearing in New York in the Chapter 11 proceeding, into which he "transposed" his findings in the Vermont adversary proceeding, including the prima facie finding of fraud. Davis, Polk on behalf of Bankers Trust, and Sullivan & Cromwell on behalf of O'Melveny and Adam Harris moved in the Southern District of New York and simultaneously in the District of Vermont for a stay of Judge Conrad's order directing the turnover of privileged documents, for leave to appeal that order to the District Court and for a writ of mandamus vacating the portions of the order discussed above.

Although we had suggested that Judge John Martin of the Southern District of New York defer to Judge Fred Parker of the District of Vermont, Judge Martin was the first to rule. Even before Judge Martin issued his decision, all parties to the Vermont sanctions proceeding agreed to be bound by whatever ruling Judge Martin made. Judge Martin proceeded to issue an opinion squarely holding that the facts before the Bankruptcy Court "did not establish probable cause to believe that Bankers had been guilty of a crime or fraud" and that "[n]othing in the record indicates that Bankers attempted to mislead the court or its adversaries about the state of its knowledge of the location of St. Johnsbury's records." Judge Martin accordingly issued a writ of mandamus directing Judge Conrad to vacate the provisions of his order terminating Bankers Trust's and O'Melveny's privileges. That should have been an end to the matter, but regrettably it wasn't.

Counsel for Clifford, having been rebuffed by Judge Martin in the Southern District of New York, disregarded his undertaking to be bound by Judge Martin's ruling and moved in the Vermont adversary proceeding for an order requiring that documents claimed by Bankers Trust and O'Melveny to be privileged be submitted for in camera review. Judge Conrad astonishingly granted the motion in an opinion that exhibited extraordinary disrespect for Judge Martin's order, by which Judge Conrad was bound. "We are in Vermont now," he announced, so Judge Martin's decision was "without effect on this proceeding...." Not content with that ruling, Judge Conrad went on to state that Judge Martin's decision "confuses 'fraud' with 'fraud on the court'...," as though "fraud" were a chameleon concept.

Judge Conrad summarily dismissed Bankers Trust's claim that it had relied on Clifford's representation concerning the location of accounts receivable records. I strongly suspect that many lawyers in my firm and elsewhere would be surprised by Judge Conrad's "hold[ing] that it is, within the legal profession, conventionally preposterous for a lender to claim that it relied on the borrower to determine where to perfect its security interest."

Judge Conrad concluded that "[b]ased on our own litigation experience, our knowledge of the standards of the bar, and our familiarity with these proceedings…we find that there exists reasonable cause to believe that the Bankers Trust counterclaim in the adversary proceeding was filed for an objectively unreasonable purpose"—in flat contradiction to Judge Martin's ruling quoted above.[11]

Judge Conrad proceeded to direct that all documents claimed by Bankers Trust and O'Melveny to be privileged be submitted for in camera review by a senior bankruptcy judge. Yet having ordered an in camera review, Judge Conrad reversed course without explanation two months later in a memorandum decision directing that "all privileged matters be turned over to Sanctions Counsel [i.e., Clifford's counsel] forthwith." The District Court in Vermont stayed that order till the in camera review was completed.

By this point, any reader must be scratching her head wondering what was going on. I can only say that the Davis Polk lawyers for Bankers Trust, Marty Glenn at O'Melveny and I as that firm's counsel, were just as baffled. To order

---

[11] Judge Conrad's inflated ego suffuses his opinion. He uses the royal "we" time and again, as in the sanctimonious statement that "we are raised in our profession to play certain games by certain rules"—as though a fraud claim asserted against a law firm were a "game."

that documents be turned over to opposing counsel, then that they be submitted for in camera review, and then reiterate the turnover order simply made no sense. Indeed, Judge John Murtha of the District Court in Vermont observed in a later decision that he could "discern no reason" for those inconsistent directives.

In connection with a subsequent hearing on the sanctions motion, I retained Geoffrey C. Hazard, Jr., an acknowledged expert on legal ethics, to express an opinion on O'Melveny's conduct. Professor Hazard submitted an affidavit opining that O'Melveny had not had a conflict of interest in representing Bankers Trust in asserting the counterclaim against Clifford. Shortly after that hearing, exhaustion prevailed; the adversary proceeding was settled; and a revised plan of reorganization was approved.

It was rewarding to work with Bob Fiske and his colleagues and, as I've said, a joy to have Marty Glenn as a client representative. But it was—and remains—equally disturbing to have appeared before a judge who treated his court like a fiefdom. I was not surprised to learn that when Judge Conrad's ten-year term on the Bankruptcy Court expired, he was not reappointed.

25

ARBITRATIONS

In the final years of my tenure as partner and in the ensuing twelve years I have been Of Counsel to the Firm, I have served as an arbitrator roughly ten times (not counting my service on the pro bono arbitration panel of the District Court for the Eastern District of New York). Inasmuch as arbitration is a confidential method of dispute resolution frequently chosen over court litigation in whole or in part for that very reason, I am constrained in what I can say about specific arbitrations. But without disclosing the identity of the parties, I want to recount briefly two arbitration experiences and believe I can do so without violating any obligation to maintain confidentiality.

In the first I represented a party to an arbitration in which Griffin Bell sat as sole arbitrator. (Griffin Bell was always referred to in his later years as "Judge Bell" because he had sat on the United States Court of Appeals for the Fifth Circuit for fourteen years before serving as Attorney-General under President Carter.) I had briefly met Judge Bell during a meeting of the American College of Trial Lawyers, but he did not remember me, nor was there any reason he should have.

The arbitration hearing was convened in Los Angeles. As Judge Bell was eager to return to his Atlanta office, he informed counsel that we would sit from 9 a.m. to 6 p.m. every day, and so we did for three days, amassing a transcript of nearly 900 pages. The hearing was particularly challenging because Judge Bell had the most pronounced Southern accent I had ever heard. When he ruled on an objection or asked a question, it was imperative that you understand him, but sometimes it was nearly impossible to do so. The arbitration was also unique in my experience in that Judge Bell brought with him an associate from his firm, King & Spaulding, to serve as the equivalent of a law clerk.

Testimony ended in the early afternoon of the third day. Judge Bell then heard oral argument from counsel, during which he peppered both my adversary and me with penetrating questions that demonstrated that he had not only listened carefully to the testimony, but also had a complete grasp of the issues. Two or three months later he rendered his decision in a thirteen-page opinion in which there was neither a wasted word nor an errant observation.

* * *

The other arbitration deserving mention was a high-stakes dispute between a large industrial company and a reinsurer. The arbitration hearing was conducted in London. I was serving as president of the American College of Trial Lawyers at the time and could not afford to spend very much time away from the duties of that position, so taking a leaf from Judge Bell's book, I proposed that we sit from 9 a.m. to 5 p.m. To my surprise, counsel and the other arbitrators agreed.

Lead counsel for the reinsurance company was Jonathan Sumption, a barrister of whom I had never heard. I had read the pre-hearing submissions of the parties and formed a tentative view that the insured was entitled to prevail on the merits. Sumption's presentation, both his examination of witnesses and his oral argument, turned me completely around. His arguments were so compelling that it was almost as though I had no freedom of thought. The panel eventually ruled for his client. Small wonder that Sumption had been appointed Queen's Counsel at the relatively young age of thirty-eight.

I later learned that in addition to being a brilliant barrister, Jonathan Sumption had written the definitive multivolume history of the Hundred Years War between England and France. I was not surprised when he was appointed to the newly established Supreme Court of England and Wales directly from the Bar without serving as a trial or intermediate appellate judge—for which to my knowledge there was no precedent.

PART IV: EVERY MAN A DEBTOR TO HIS PROFESSION[12]

Ever since I was admitted to the bar, I have considered Sir Francis Bacon's legendary statement about a lawyer's duty to his profession to be a beacon guiding my professional career. I have sought to fulfill that exhortation in many different ways, of which I will discuss only three here: (1) my tenure as president of the New York City Bar Association (formerly The Association of the Bar of the City of New York), (2) my presidency of the American College of Trial Lawyers, and (3) my service as chair of the New York Lawyer Assistance Trust.

[12] Francis Bacon, Sr., famously wrote: "I hold every man a debtor to his profession; from the which as men of course do seek to receive countenance and profit, so ought they of duty to endeavor themselves by way of amends to be a help and ornament thereunto."

26

NEW YORK CITY BAR ASSOCIATION

Though I cannot recall the year in which I joined the New York City Bar Association, it must have been not long after I started work at Sullivan & Cromwell, for I was invited in or about 1962 by our partner Roy Steyer, then Chair of the Trade Regulation Committee, to become committee secretary. It was a tradition at the Association in those years that when a partner in a large law firm was appointed to chair a committee, he would invite one of his younger colleagues to serve as committee secretary to attend to ministerial duties.

The next bar association committee of which I recall being a member was the Professional and Judicial Ethics Committee. Steve Kaye of the Proskauer firm had become chair of that committee in 1985. When Steve assumed the position, he found that the committee had accumulated a long list of unanswered inquiries. It was impractical to attempt to respond to each with a closely reasoned opinion with citations, as had been the committee's tradition. Steve's eminently sensible solution to the problem was to divide the inquiries into two groups: (1) those which were highly fact-specific and did not provide suitable opportunities to give generalized guidance to lawyers as to future conduct, and (2) those which did lend themselves to giving such guidance. The former, Steve concluded, should be addressed with brief responses, leaving the latter for more elaborate treatment including citations to earlier ethics committee opinions and court decisions.

When Steve's term ended, I succeeded him as committee chair. It was my prerogative to recommend new members to the Association president. Surveying the committee roster,

I noted that there were no members over the age of sixty, leaving the committee without an important perspective. I cured that omission by recommending Justin Feldman, a partner in the Kronish Lieb firm. Justin brought wisdom as well as experience to the committee. Justin and his wife, the noted sex crimes prosecutor and novelist Linda Fairstein, had a home on Martha's Vineyard, as my wife Nan and I did and still do, and that common tie deepened my friendship with Justin.

In 1993 I was elected to the Association's executive committee, on which I served for three years as a member and a fourth as chair. In addition to its policy-making functions, the executive committee formulated the Association's stated position on nominations to the Supreme Court of the United States. The executive committee took that responsibility very seriously. For example, when Justice Breyer's nomination was pending, I spoke to all of my partners who had appeared before him as a judge of the Court of Appeals for the First Circuit, and lawyers in my firm reviewed and prepared a report on the fourteen opinions he had written in antitrust cases.

Immediately after my service on the executive committee, I was elected a vice-president of the Association, and the following year I was elected president. I held that office for two years: 1998–99 and 1999–2000. It was humbling to realize that I was the first Sullivan & Cromwell partner to serve as president in the entire 120-year history of the Association. My predecessor, Michael Cardozo, had left very big shoes to fill. In addition to a keen mind, Michael had an enviable capacity to make difficult decisions and a seemingly bottomless reservoir of energy.

I was asked by several people whether I had a fixed agenda beginning my two-year presidential term. I responded by quoting the advice given by Hippocrates to physicians more than two thousand years ago: "*Primum non nocere.*" ("First, do no harm.")

How to describe the Association? With more than 20,000 members, it has functioned principally though committees (both standing and special) and task forces, running the full gamut of legal subjects and socio-political issues. Leafing through the pages of the Association's bi-monthly periodical, *The Record*, gives some idea of the immense range of subjects with which the Association has concerned itself: statutory time limits for guardianship hearings and decisions; electric utility restructuring in New York; aviation safety; ratification of the convention on the elimination of all forms of discrimination against women; and the proposed Product Liability Reform Act of 1998. These were in fact the subjects of the first five committee reports published in the *Record* after I became president.

The committees had differing and sometimes conflicting perspectives. One example will suffice. Shortly after I became president, the Surrogate's Court Committee asked to meet with me to discuss a recently issued report by the Government Ethics Committee drawing attention to the fact that guardianships ad litem in the Surrogate's Court, which could prove quite lucrative, were more often than not awarded to a lawyer who had contributed to the election campaign of the appointing judge. The Government Ethics Committee decried this example of "pay-to-play." When I met with the Surrogate's Court Committee, its chair told me that the Government Ethics Committee had inappropriately encroached on the province of the Surrogate's Court Committee. I was both bemused and offended by this myopic attitude, but it gave me fair warning of jurisdictional disputes to come. Needless to say, the

Government Ethics Committee report was not withdrawn. To the contrary, the Association successfully called on the ABA and the New York State Bar Association to condemn the practice of "pay-to-play."

At the beginning of the Association year following the Annual Meeting in May, the president traditionally met with all committee chairs, an almost herculean task when one recalls that there were more than fifty committees. It took me a while, but I succeeded in discharging that responsibility. Having observed that older, retired lawyers remained interested in committee work, I appointed a few as committee chairs. It was also the custom then—I don't know whether it still is—that the president reviewed each committee report before it was issued, and I dutifully adhered to that custom, even though the subject matter of reports was occasionally beyond my knowledge.

The Association has long had a resolute commitment to diversity in the profession. In 1991 the Association issued a Statement of Goals on the Recruitment and Retention of Minorities; that statement was reissued while I was President. We created programs to encourage minority youth to consider a career in the law, as well as programs for minority law students. We also reached out to, and sought opportunities to collaborate with, minority bar associations.

In the spring of 1998, the Association issued (later than we should have) a similar Statement on the Recruitment and Retention of Women. For many years the Association has appointed women as committee chairs, and it currently has its fourth woman President: Deborah Raskin, who follows Barbara Paul Robinson, Betsy Plevan, and Pat Hynes.

The Association has always been mindful of its responsibilities to its members, which it fulfills in many ways. The Association library has a vast collection accessible to all of its members, as well as to judges and (according to its By-laws) to the President of the United States. Shortly after I became Association president, New York promulgated a strict continuing legal education (CLE) requirement: as a condition of remaining in good standing, an attorney was required (and still is) to take twenty-four credit hours of approved CLE every two years. To assist attorneys in meeting this requirement, the Association ramped up its CLE Department, including opening a new 130-seat CLE Training Center with state-of-the-art audiovisual equipment.

For those of its members who practice alone or in small firms, the Association created a Small Law Firm Center, providing networking opportunities and helping members to procure computer hardware and software. Finally, acknowledging the fact that life in the law is a continuum, while I was President the Association created a law student member category and publicized its availability to the thousands of law students in the thirteen accredited law schools in the Metropolitan New York area.

The Association has long had close ties to the state and federal judiciary in New York. Judge Michael Sonberg of the Bronx County Criminal Court was Secretary of the Association during my presidential term, and Justices Richard Andrias of the Appellate Division, First Department, and Barry Cozier of the Supreme Court, New York County, were members of the Executive Committee. Several years after my term as President, Barry Kamins, a distinguished criminal defense lawyer in Brooklyn and a former Judge of the Criminal Court, became president.

The Association's interests have extended to all levels of government. At the municipal level, for example, the Association closely monitored the work of the Charter Revision Commission created by Mayor Giuliani and publicly commented on the commission's proposals. For many years, the Association has similarly monitored and commented on proposed legislation in the New York State Senate and Assembly.

The Association also looks outward to the international community. During my term as president, the Association participated in celebrating the 50th anniversary of the Universal Declaration of Human Rights with Senator George J. Mitchell as the keynote speaker. And as president of the Association I was invited to attend the annual opening of the French courts, known as the Rentrée, in Paris. The Association's focus on international affairs takes many forms. In 1998 the Association hosted a reception for legal advisors to UN member nations. During my term as President, the Senate Foreign Relations Committee, chaired by Senator Jesse Helms, held a hearing at the Association on the United States' obligation to contribute to the UN budget. I greeted Senator Helms at the entrance to the building and escorted him to the Meeting Hall. It was a bit surreal to see Senator Helms wielding a gavel sitting in the chair I usually occupied.

The Association is always vibrant with energy. If you visit it any day around 7 p.m., you will find committee meetings being held in each of the meeting rooms named after past presidents and other legal luminaries (including William Nelson Cromwell), as well as throngs entering the meeting hall to hear a lecture. It is natural to assume that this hubbub of activity runs effortlessly over rails laid decades ago. But, of course, that is not true. The Association must be continuously managed and overseen like any other large and complicated enterprise. When I became president, that management and oversight were provided by Barbara Berger Opotowsky, who had succeeded Fern Schair as executive director one year earlier. Hiring Barbara may well have been Michael Cardozo's greatest contribution to the Association as president. During her fifteen-year tenure as executive director, Barbara brought to all of her manifold responsibilities a level of intelligence, competence, judgment, and infectious enthusiasm that were unequalled in my experience. Barbara was simply a joy to work with, and we became close personal friends. I sometimes think of Barbara as the sister I never had.

Alongside Barbara as the second anchor of the Association was Alan Rothstein, General Counsel. Alan, who held that position for two decades until his retirement last year, was a font of knowledge of all of the Association's past and present. I don't think I have ever asked Alan a question to which he did not have an answer, if not at his fingertips, then within a few minutes of research. Alan was devoid of ego; he was there to help the Association run as smoothly as possible. I was and remain in his debt, as is every Association member.

No description of the Association would be complete without mention of the public service programs run by the City Bar Fund (since renamed the City Bar Justice Center) under the inspired leadership of Maria Imperiale and her equally inspired successor, Lynn Kelly. The City Bar Justice Center has helped to connect the Association membership to the poor and needy among us, and it played a crucial role in helping to mobilize lawyer volunteers after 9/11.

Shortly after my election as president, I was invited to have lunch with the Justices of the Appellate Division, First Department. I was seated to the right of the Presiding Justice, Alfred Lerner, and during a lull in the conversation, I asked whether the Court had ever considered a diversionary program for lawyers charged with disciplinary wrongdoing whose misconduct was rooted in alcoholism or other substance abuse. Though the answer appeared to be no, Justice Lerner expressed keen interest in the subject.[12] I recall him noting that when he had served in the Supreme Court, Queens County, there were a few lawyers who, if their cases were called after lunch, would exhibit symptoms of having imbibed to excess. He added ruefully that he would arrange it so that the cases of these lawyers were always called in the morning. Only later did he realize that he had enabled their alcohol abuse.

Whether or not he was motivated in part by guilt, Justice Lerner strongly urged me to have the Association address this issue. In the following weeks, he kept after me, but I needed little persuading that this was an issue the Association should address. And address it we did by creating a Lawyer Assistance Program ("LAP") to provide counseling, referral, intervention, and peer support to lawyers, judges, and law students. The program addresses not only alcohol and substance abuse, but also depression, anxiety, and other mental health issues.

We chose wisely in appointing Eileen Travis to head the program. She has continued in that position since the program's creation in May 1999. When I last checked with Eileen in October 2014, she told me that during its fifteen-year existence, the LAP had provided direct services (evaluation, assessment, counseling, referral, and peer support) to 3,530 attorneys, judges, law students, and their family members. It has also provided educational presentations at

---

[12] The New York State disciplinary process was recently revised to incorporate a provision authorizing referral to diversionary programs of lawyers accused of unethical conduct that is rooted in alcohol or other substance abuse—one of the last of many salutary reforms instituted by retiring Chief Judge Jonathan Lippman.

bar associations, judicial seminars, CLE programs, law firms, law schools, and nonprofit agencies to 72,000 participants in New York City. I find those numbers both astonishing and reassuring. All or most of this reform might have happened eventually; it happened when it did because of my impromptu lunchtime conversation with Justice Lerner at the Appellate Division and his persistent follow-up and also because of the extraordinary efforts of Eileen Travis.

From time to time, but not often, the Association bestows honorary membership on an individual. During my tenure as president, Chief Justice William H. Rehnquist was chosen to receive that honor. He addressed a packed Meeting Hall on April 13, 1999. It was my privilege to present the certificate of honorary membership to him.

I had earlier presented a similar certificate to George Mitchell when he was awarded honorary membership for his singular contributions in shaping the Good Friday Accords that ended decades of bloodshed in Northern Ireland.

Another of the president's responsibilities was to select the speakers for the signature lectures at the Association, of which the most prestigious is the Cardozo Lecture. Some of the speakers in that fifty-year-old lecture series were monumental figures in the law, such as United States Supreme Court Justices Robert H. Jackson and Felix Frankfurter and Judge Henry Friendly of the U.S. Court of Appeals for the Second Circuit. During my first year as president, Justice Ruth Bader Ginsburg agreed to deliver the lecture and did so on February 11, 1999, in a packed meeting hall. In my introduction, I referred to Justice Ginsburg as "one of our own." However presumptuous that reference may have appeared, it was justified, for not only had she been a member of the Association, she had served on its executive committee from 1974 to 1978.

MAC Presentation to Chief Justice William Rehnquist (New York City Bar Association)

The first tenured woman on the Columbia Law School faculty, Ruth Bader Ginsburg had founded the Women's Rights Project at the ACLU and argued or submitted amicus curiae (literally "friend of the court") briefs in six cases involving gender discrimination before the Supreme Court of the United States. She was commonly thought of as an advocate of women's rights, but she also pursued the goal of eradicating unjustifiable gender distinctions, whether they favored men or women.[13] I vividly recall her Cardozo Lecture, which was entitled "Affirmative Action: An International Human Rights Dialogue." Not only was every seat taken in the large Meeting Hall of the Association, young women lawyers, law students, and just plain admirers sat on the floor in the rows separating seats. What a tribute to a Justice who will surely reside in the pantheon of great Supreme Court Justices.

The following year I wished to invite Anthony Lewis to give the Cardozo Lecture for reasons I will explain in a moment, but I was concerned that he might not qualify because while he frequently wrote about the law, he was not himself a lawyer, although he had spent one year at Harvard Law School as a Niemann Fellow. I retrieved from the Association's archives the minutes of the 1951 Executive Committee meeting at which the lectureship was created, and was relieved to find that the resolution creating the lectureship specified that the lecture be *about* the law, but said nothing about the qualifications of the lecturer. I proceeded to invite Anthony Lewis to give the lecture; he accepted the invitation and delivered the lecture on January 16, 2000.

I will digress for a moment to say something about Tony

---

[13] Why, she asked in one case, should a woman be able to purchase 3.2 percent beer in Oklahoma at the age of eighteen when a man had to wait till the age of twenty-one? Or why should women be exempt from jury service on request when men were not similarly favored?

Lewis and also about an individual to whom he introduced me on the evening of his Cardozo Lecture. I first encountered Tony Lewis when I read *Gideon's Trumpet*, his account of the celebrated case of *Gideon v. Wainwright*, in which the Supreme Court recognized a constitutional right to counsel for any individual charged with a serious crime. The case reached the Supreme Court via a handwritten petition for certiorari penned by Clarence Gideon, an uneducated Floridian. It is true that the subject matter of the book was compelling in and of itself, but Tony Lewis told the saga of Gideon's journey to the Supreme Court in elegantly simple yet moving prose. I had also read and greatly enjoyed a number of the columns, each headed "At Home Abroad," he had written for the *New York Times* when stationed in its London office.

Tony Lewis and I continued in contact after he delivered the Cardozo Lecture, and we formed a friendship, aided by the fact that we both had homes on Martha's Vineyard and aided also by the delight Nan and I felt in befriending Tony's partner in life, Margie Marshall, the twenty-fourth and first woman Chief Judge of the Massachusetts Supreme Judicial Court. Margie is best known for her landmark decision in *Goodrich v. Department of Public Health*, the first state supreme court decision upholding the constitutional right of same-sex couples to marry. Margie is not one-dimensional: she was a student leader of the anti-apartheid movement in South Africa and is the Senior Fellow of the Yale Corporation.

An oft-paid compliment is that an individual is "good company." Well, Tony Lewis was simply the *best* company: a superb writer, thoughtful commentator, engaging conversationalist, good listener, and caring friend. I will never forget the day in August 2009 when I lay in bed in Massachusetts General Hospital recovering from surgery and opened my eyes to see Tony entering my room. He was eighty-two years old and in poor health. He had driven from Cambridge to visit me on hearing that I was hospitalized. I could not fathom how, with his stooped back, he was able to see over the hood of his car, but he had somehow managed. His visit brightened my day.

I last saw Tony Lewis when I was in Cambridge for a meeting at Harvard Law School in October 2012. Though he was physically frail, his mind was as keen as ever, and he was a gracious host. Five months later, he passed away, just a few days after giving a talk at Brandeis University on the 50th anniversary of *Gideon v. Wainwright.* What a farewell!

Shortly before Tony Lewis was to give the Cardozo Lecture at the Association, he called to ask whether he could bring to the pre-lecture dinner a friend who was visiting from London. I, of course, readily assented even before learning the friend's name, and that is how I met Sydney Kentridge, who had moved to London after a celebrated career as a barrister in South Africa.

Having been a junior member of the team of barristers representing Nelson Mandela in the 1950s, Sydney was retained by the widow and mother of Stephen Biko, an anti-apartheid leader who died in prison in 1977 after a fall (or so the authorities claimed, though his family and others believed, and there was evidence suggesting, that a vicious beating caused his death). At the ensuing coroner's inquest, at which according to South African law and custom the family of the deceased was entitled to be represented by counsel, who had the right to examine witnesses, Sydney Kentridge's cross-examination of the prison chief of police was so devastating and gripping that the proceeding was turned into a stage drama and portions of his cross-examination were quoted word for word.

After moving to London, Sydney Kentridge established himself as a barrister of choice. We became friends, aided by the proximity of his country home in Lewes to the Brighton house in which my daughter Sarah and her family then lived. When Tony Lewis died, Sydney flew from London to speak at the memorial service organized by Margie Marshall at Harvard's Memorial Church. Sydney's remembrance of Tony, delivered soon after he arrived from London, was the only one spoken without notes.

Sydney Kentridge was so renowned and revered as a barrister that the Supreme Court of England and Wales set one of his cases for argument on Sydney's ninetieth birthday! I last saw Sydney in September 2014 when the American College of Trial Lawyers met in London. As an Honorary Fellow of the College, Sydney was invited to attend the two morning programs. He listened attentively through both three-hour-long programs, and after the first he joined Nan and me for lunch. He was remarkably alert and articulate for someone approaching his ninety-second birthday, and we had a wonderful leisurely lunch.

I consider myself blessed to have known and befriended Tony Lewis, Margie Marshall, and Sydney Kentridge.

I could not possibly have carried out all of my duties as Association president without the generous and complete support of Sullivan & Cromwell. Although the time I could devote to client matters was reduced substantially, my compensation was not affected one penny, so far as I could determine. I doubt many other law firms would have been so generous. Moreover, the firm at its own cost made the technological changes and connections that permitted me to work on client matters in my Association office as though I were physically present at my 125 Broad Street law firm office.

One unanticipated benefit of my City Bar presidency was

the opportunity to get to know Evan Davis, a Cleary partner who succeeded me. Evan had contracted poliomyelitis as a youth and has ever since been confined to a wheelchair. That dependence has not prevented Evan from scaling the heights of our profession.

During his year as president, Evan invited me and Loretta Lynch, at the time United States Attorney for the Eastern District of New York and now United States Attorney-General, to join him on a trip to Johannesburg, South Africa, where we were scheduled to interview young black South African lawyers for positions as interns at New York City law firms and corporate law departments. The goal was to expose them to issues of New York and international commercial law so that they might return to South Africa with additional qualifications for advanced positions in their law firms.

The trip was lengthy—seventeen hours nonstop—and exhausting, but we immediately went to work. The three of us were joined by three black South African interviewers: a dynamic young woman law firm partner whose name I cannot now recall, Justice Anthony Madala of the South Africa Supreme Court, and Justice Dikgang Moseneke, who at the time presided at the High Court in Pretoria.

Justice Moseneke is truly the most charismatic individual I have ever met, and his life story is the stuff of legend. He had been imprisoned by the apartheid regime when he was fifteen years old for supposedly leading a student rebellion and had spent ten years at the infamous Robben Island prison. There, to his great good fortune, Nelson Mandela took the youth under his wing. Moseneke received a bachelor of arts degree and then a law degree by taking correspondence classes while imprisoned. After his release he qualified as a barrister, then left the bar to become an industrial leader (Chairman of the African Merchant Bank and of Telekom SA), and eventually returned to the law when he was appointed to the High Court in Pretoria.[14]

The three South Africans, Evan, Loretta, and I conducted our interviews in a conference room at the Johannesburg airport. The young lawyers we interviewed were all thirsting for knowledge so that they might advance in the profession. They came from Johannesburg, Capetown, and as far away as Durban. I had the impression that some of the men were wearing the only suit they owned. Several were briefly tongue-tied on seeing Justice Moseneke. After the interviews concluded, we made our selections. The South African internship program has continued, and I am proud to say that Sullivan & Cromwell has participated in it.

[14] In 2002, the year after I met Justice Moseneke, he was elevated by then-President Thabo Mbeki to the South Africa Constitutional Court, where he is now Deputy Chief Justice. I have read reports that he would have been appointed Chief Justice but for the fact that Justice Moseneke is reportedly aligned with the Mbeki-led opposition wing of the governing party now led by President Jacob Azuma. Justice Moseneke is also Chancellor of the University of the Witwatersrand, the leading university in South Africa.

27

AMERICAN COLLEGE OF TRIAL LAWYERS

When I was elected to fellowship in the American College of Trial Lawyers in 1977, I knew little about the College, but I soon learned and became immersed in its history, qualifications, mission, and activities.

It is accepted lore that the idea of forming an organization of the most skilled trial advocates came one night to a California lawyer named Emil Gumpert while he was restlessly lying in an upper berth on a train headed from Stockton, California, to Los Angeles in April 1950. During the ensuing year he recruited a few other lawyers and then brashly invited the President of the American Bar Association, Cody Fowler of Tampa, Florida, to address the group. In 1952 Fowler was elected president of the College, and he was reelected two years later. Over the next decade, some of the giants of the trial bar, including Albert E. Jenner, Jr., Leon Jaworski, Robert Meserve, and Whitney North Seymour, served as president. With these luminaries successively heading the College, it slowly achieved national recognition as an organization of the "best of the best" trial lawyers.

Emil Gumpert authored a "charge" that is delivered to new inductees at the College's national meetings. The charge is written in archaic, flowery prose, but it has never failed to move me. Its central metaphor of "the hermit and the horse," borrowed from the great English jurist, Lord Eldon, somehow captures the life of the trial lawyer, evoking both the solitary hours of preparation and the great effort that a trial lawyer's life entails. Emil Gumpert delivered the charge at each national meeting until his death in 1983. Since then, the charge has been delivered by a past president, and it was my privilege to do so in September 2014 when the College met in London.

From the outset, fellowship has been limited to those lawyers who are "outstanding," "unquestionably and eminently qualified," and "actively engaged in trial work as their principal activity." The College considers the "totality" of a lawyer's adversarial experience—not limited to trials on the merits, but including all "adversarial proceedings" such as preliminary injunction hearings. Some years ago, there was much discussion at a board of regents meeting of a candidate proposed by then regent (and later president) Ed Brodsky of New York. The candidate had only three or four trials under his belt, but they were very lengthy and exceedingly complicated antitrust trials. No one with that few trials had theretofore been admitted to fellowship in the College, but after a lengthy discussion, the board of regents decided to approve the candidate under what then became known as the "Brodsky exception."

As the number of trials held throughout the country has diminished due to, among other causes, increased client sensitivity to the costs of trials and trial preparation and to the rise of mediation and arbitration as alternative forms of dispute resolution, the College has been faced with accepting the probability of considering fewer nominees and addressed the issue in 2006 by amending the Statement of Qualifications to permit consideration of appellate experience as a "favorable factor," to codify the Brodsky exception to take into account the complexity as well as the number of trials, and to accept as qualifying "trials" both arbitrations and contested administrative proceedings.

Nominees for fellowship may be proposed by a Fellow with a seconding Fellow. However, a Fellow may not propose or second the proposal of his or her partner. A nominee may also be taken up by a state or province committee on its own motion, and in the infrequent case of a lawyer who tries cases principally outside the geographic area of his or her primary office, the nomination is considered in the first instance by the Adjunct State Committee.

If the State, Province, or Adjunct State Committee approves a nominee, the regent for that jurisdiction (there are fifteen in all) conducts a separate examination of the nominee's qualifications, including direct contact with opposing counsel, counsel for co-parties, and the judges before whom the nominee has tried cases. The regent then presents his or her nominees to the entire board of regents at one of the College's semiannual meetings, including a recommendation as to whether the nomination should or should not be approved. I can assure you from many years' experience that the presenting regent is subjected to questioning as searching as any he or she has experienced in a courtroom.

The College is "dedicated," according to the very first section of its bylaws, "to maintaining and improving the standards of trial practice, the administration of justice, and the ethics of the profession." In support of that tripartite mission, the College has issued two "Codes," one governing trial conduct and the other pretrial conduct. Chief Justice John G. Roberts, Jr., has written a short letter commending the Codes to all lawyers, as did his predecessor, Chief Justice William H. Rehnquist.

The College has also issued two "manuals," one on mass tort litigation and the other on U.S.-Canada cross-border civil litigation and practice. Notable committee reports and "white papers" have covered such diverse subjects as the attorney-client privilege, contested judicial elections (which the College is on record as opposing), and discovery in civil cases, the last a joint project of the College and the Institute for the Advancement of the American Legal System.

The College's broadly stated mission, particularly that part pledging to further "the administration of justice," is open to varying interpretations. Always mindful that the College is "not another bar association," the regents occasionally disagree as to whether the College should place its name on a project, such as the filing of an amicus brief.

Roughly once a decade, the board of regents holds a retreat to consider the scope of appropriate activities for the College, the qualifications for fellowship, governance issues, and any other subject the Retreat Planning Committee thinks appropriate. The first retreat I attended was in May 2002. I chaired the retreat planning committee responsible for governance issues, which submitted an eighteen-page report with recommendations. The most recent retreat was held in the summer of 2015. These retreats, which last two days, provide an essential opportunity for self-examination and thoughtful discussion of ways to improve the College's governance and activities and to expand its profile in suitable ways.

The College operates thorough committees, both state or province committees and "general" committees. The scope of activities of the latter committees varies widely. The National Trial Competition Committee sponsors, in conjunction with the Texas Young Lawyers, a nationwide competition with elimination rounds in each region followed by a final round in Texas. (I presided over the final round trial when I was College president in 2005–06.) A parallel competition, the Sopinka Cup, is administered by the Canadian Fellows of the College.

The National Moot Court Competition Committee also sponsors a national competition, this one in collaboration with the Young Lawyers Committee of the New York City

Bar Association. I have sat as a judge in the semifinal round of that competition for many years and, ex officio when I was president of that Association, on the bench for the final round. I have been amazed each year by the forensic abilities and preparation of the student advocates and their adeptness in fielding questions from the bench that are not always clearly stated or directly on point. Again, there is a parallel competition, the Gale Cup, in Canada.

The crown jewel all the general committees in my view is the Emil Gumpert Award Committee, named after the founder of the College. At its origin and for several years, the award was given to a law school to encourage the teaching of trial advocacy. Eventually that subject became so widely a part of the law school curriculum that the board of regents decided in or about 2005 to change the recipient to an organization dedicated, as is the College, to maintaining and improving the administration of justice. Perhaps at least in part because the award is accompanied by a substantial monetary stipend, originally $50,000 and now $100,000, the Emil Gumpert Award Committee receives many applications, all of which are carefully scrutinized. When the number is narrowed down to three or four, a team of committee members visits each of the finalist organizations to meet with its leaders and form a direct impression of its operations. The committee then selects an applicant to recommend to the board of regents and accompanies its recommendation with a report discussing all the finalists and detailing the reasons for its recommendation.

The board of regents has accepted the committee's recommendation without exception and forwarded it, with the Board's approval, to the College foundation, which funds the award. The Gumpert Award has been given to organizations serving a wide range of disadvantaged populations, ranging from immigrants and refugees to children seeking resentencing, victims of human trafficking, and the elderly.

The College does not run automatically. Like the New York City Bar Association, the College requires a steady hand at the administrative helm. Fortunately, for more than a decade Dennis Maggi has been the executive director of the College. Like most successful administrative heads, Dennis operates quietly and effectively. I marvel at how smoothly the fall annual meeting and the spring meeting are conducted. Dennis responds almost instantaneously to requests and inquiries, and I cannot recall ever seeing a frown on his face.

I have to this point described the structure, operations, governance, and committee activity of the College, but have not said what it has meant to me personally to be a Fellow. Although my practice had taken me to state and federal courts in many jurisdictions and provided an opportunity to meet many trial lawyers across the Nation and Canada, I have nevertheless lived in a New York–centric world. But through the College, particularly during my year as president, I have met and befriended interesting and collegial Fellows from virtually every state and province.

To give but one example, I vividly recall encountering at an early meeting I attended a warm and cordial Fellow from Tallahassee named Carl R. Pennington, Jr. Our backgrounds, non-legal interests, and accents could not have been more different. Carl lived for fly-fishing, which I have done once and failed at, and his accent was as thick as grade A molasses. But we shared a passion for trial advocacy and enjoyed meeting other advocates, and that passion and collegiality were a sufficient foundation for a friendship. That is but one of many friendships I have formed with trial advocates in the United States and Canada whom I otherwise would not have met. Of all the benefits I have enjoyed while a Fellow of the

College, the opportunity to form and cultivate those friendships has been the most precious.

In 2000 Bob Fiske, a good friend and past president of the College, asked me whether I would be interested in serving as a regent. I answered "yes" in a heartbeat. Jim Stapleton, the regent for our region, consisting of New York, Connecticut, and Vermont, was ending his term, and in due course I was chosen to succeed him. I must admit to having been intimidated initially when I attended board meetings, particularly when I had to present candidates for the first time. At the spring board meeting in 2002, I was sitting at my assigned chair when Earl Silbert, the junior past president, entered the room and quietly asked me to join him outside. He told me that the Officers Nominating Committee, that is to say, all of the past presidents in attendance, had just voted to elect me as the next secretary. I was stunned, because I had served only two years of my four-year term as regent. I accepted, of course, and then returned to the board meeting. After I had served as secretary for one year, I was elected treasurer, the following year president-elect and the year after that president.

My year as president was nothing short of a whirlwind. I traveled almost continuously from Maine to Hawaii and from Alberta to Mexico. I made forty-eight trips to forty-three cities and towns in thirty-one states and Canadian provinces. I flew to Honolulu for the annual dinner of the Hawaii Fellows and thence to a small town on the west coast of Mexico, where *mirabile dictu* the Oklahoma Fellows met biennially because Fellow Terry West from Shawnee had a gorgeous hillside home there. Twice I visited two states on a single trip: first Washington and Oregon, and then Louisiana and Mississippi. My wife Nan accompanied me on most of these trips. I was grateful for her company at the time, but

ACTL Board of Regents Spring 2006 (ACTL)

do not understand to this day how she could spare the time from her archaeological pursuits at Barnard, where she was a tenured professor.

The physical toll of all that travel and the responsibilities of the presidency were enormous, particularly because I managed somehow to squeeze in a three-week arbitration hearing in London. I finally reached the point in August where I simply needed a breather and, therefore, asked one of the other executive committee members to stand in for me at the Iowa Fellows annual dinner. That, I believe, is the only "free" weekend I had during the entire year.

Of all the places I visited, two stand out: the Mexico trip I've already mentioned and the regional meeting of the Northwest Fellows in Medora, North Dakota, a town of which I had never heard but which achieved fame because Teddy Roosevelt retreated there to heal after the deaths of his wife and mother. To commemorate him, a large outdoor arena was carved into a hillside, and every year people gather from all over the Northwest to see a musical show celebrating the history of the region.

While I was in Medora, I stole a few hours one morning to go horseback riding. I somehow found myself in the company of two young girls. When the three of us reached the ranch where we were going to ride, the foreman asked whether any of us had experience horseback riding. I raised my hand because I had ridden for eight years near our weekend home in the northern Westchester community of North Salem and in fact had purchased a horse in 2004. The foreman, on seeing my raised hand, said: "Put him on John." I mounted a large four-legged creature and, facing forward, noticed that his ears pointed outward at a roughly 45-degree angle. After a moment I realized that they had put me on a mule. I was a bit embarrassed (and angry, if truth be told) until I realized that for riding on the stony hillsides of the Dakota Badlands, a mule was probably a wise choice.

My year as president ended in London, where the annual meeting is held roughly once every decade. A few months before that meeting I received a handwritten letter from Lord Thomas Bingham, the senior member of the House of Lords Appellate Committee, the then English equivalent of the Supreme Court of the United States. I had never met "Tom" Bingham (as he liked to be addressed), whose letter came out of the blue. He wrote to remind me that the College's London meeting would occur on the fifth anniversary of the attack on the World Trade Center, and he offered to arrange a special memorial service at Westminster Abbey. I have never before or since received so unexpected and gracious an invitation.

When the appointed day arrived, the members of the board of regents and their spouses gathered across the street from Westminster Abbey, and Tom Bingham led us to the Abbey, stopping traffic by raising his hand. The service was extraordinarily moving, and immediately afterward I was invited to lay a wreath at the memorial to unnamed and unknown victims, the London equivalent of our Nation's Tomb of the Unknown Soldier.

Following the annual meeting in London, many of the Fellows and their guests moved on to Dublin, where a two-day conference had been arranged. Those of us on the executive committee were invited to have tea at the official residence of President Mary McAleese, a most cordial hostess, and we later attended a small dinner hosted by Chief Justice John Murray. The grand banquet the following evening was held in Dublin Castle. Afterwards we adjourned to an adjacent building, where Liam Clancy, the sole surviving member of the famed Clancy Brothers, entertained us with Irish folk music.[15] John Hume, co-architect with George Mitchell of the Good Friday Accords bringing peace to Northern Ireland and winner of the Nobel Peace Prize, who had spoken to our group earlier in the day, *sua sponte* took the stage to sing "Danny Boy" in a glorious tenor voice.

The College has had close relations with the judiciary in the United States, Canada, and England. All Justices of the United States and Canadian Supreme Courts are Honorary Fellows, as are several English jurists. The College's bond with the English bench and bar is cemented every ten or so years by an Anglo-American Exchange, in which a small group of federal and state judges and College Fellows meets in England with a similar-size group of English jurists and barristers. The visit is reciprocated the following year in the United States.

I was fortunate to be a member of the eight-person American delegation headed by Justices Antonin Scalia and Stephen Breyer in the 2004–05 Exchange. The U.K. delegation was headed by two Lords of Appeal in Ordinary, the so-called "Law Lords": Lord Scott of Foscote and Lord Rodger of Earlsferry. The U.K. delegation, which included four other judges, two barristers, and one solicitor, was led by Lord Scott, or "Richard" as he insisted on being called at the outset. He was an avid horseman and felt obliged to recuse himself when the parliamentary act outlawing the killing of foxes during fox-hunting was challenged in the courts and eventually reached the Law Lords.

In preparation for the exchanges, the College delegation

[15] The College owes a debt of gratitude to my wife Nan for Liam Clancy's presence. Nan had lived in Greenwich Village in the '60s and '70s and had heard the Clancy Brothers perform many times at the celebrated White Horse tavern. Though Liam was retired when the College went to Dublin, he accepted Nan's invitation to perform for us.

members and their U.K. counterparts have prepared papers on subjects to be discussed. My contribution in 2004 was a paper contrasting the approaches to expert testimony in the United States and U.K. courts. Heather Hallett, a Justice of the High Court, Queens Bench Division, wrote a paper on the same subject.

I cannot point to any specific impact the Anglo-American exchanges have had in the United States, but Lord Wolff has publicly credited the exchanges with providing "extremely valuable assistance" to him in shaping procedural reforms in England while he was Master of the Rolls.

I should not leave the impression that the exchange was all work and no play. We had private tours of Buckingham Palace and the Tate Modern and a lovely dinner at Jacob Rothschild's Buckinghamshire home, Waddesdon Manor, on the steps of which the accompanying photograph was taken.

I was surprised to learn during my year as president how few people knew about the American College of Trial Lawyers. That fact was brought home to me vividly when I was visiting my son Jeff in Indiana, where he is a law professor. He arranged for me to have coffee with Randall Shepard, then Chief Justice of the Indiana Supreme Court. We had a very easy and pleasant conversation, but I was astonished when he said that he knew nothing about the College. When I returned home, I drafted a four-page College brochure, with editorial assistance from Past President Ozzie Ayscue, the unofficial historian of the College and for many years editor-in-chief of the College Bulletin. The brochure was distributed to the chairs of the various state and province committees, and I urged them to send or, better yet, hand it to members of the judiciary in their respective jurisdictions. I also met with the Director of the Federal Judicial Center, Judge Barbara Rothstein. My successors have continued

ACTL 2004 Anglo-American Exchange (ACTL)

to collaborate with the FJC, including co-publication of "The Anatomy of a Patent Trial." A few years ago the College made a video for the "school" which the Federal Judicial Center conducts for newly appointed federal judges. One of the videotape segments explored the problem of how a judge should deal with a self-represented litigant. I wrote and acted in that segment, which was based on an actual case I had observed before Judge Barbara Jones in the Southern District of New York. Another outreach effort I undertook was to meet with Mary McQueen, President of the National Center for State Courts, to discuss possible collaborations between the College and her Center.

I want to turn now to what I consider the most significant action taken by the College during my years as president-elect and president: the recruitment of Fellows to serve as counsel to detainees imprisoned at the Guantanamo Bay Naval Station. But first, a bit of background.

The original detention facility at Guantanamo had been constructed hastily after passage of the congressional resolution authorizing the use of military force following the September 11, 2001, attack on the Twin Towers of the World Trade Center. Why choose Guantanamo as the site for a detention facility? Undoubtedly because Cuba had retained sovereignty when it entered into a 100-year lease of the naval station site to the United States. (The lease was renewable at our government's pleasure and has in fact been renewed.) The reasoning behind the choice of the Guantanamo site must have gone something like this: The federal courts exercise jurisdiction only in the United States, including its territories and possessions; Guantanamo Bay fell into none of those categories; ergo, the federal courts could not exercise jurisdiction over the incarceration and treatment of detainees at Guantanamo, and more particularly could not grant a writ of habeas corpus on petition by a detainee.

It took more than two years for the jurisdictional issue to reach the United States Supreme Court, which held in *Rasul v. Bush* that Section 2241 of Title 28 of the United States Code "confers [jurisdiction]on the District Court to hear petitioners' habeas corpus challenges to the legality of their detention at the Guantanamo Bay naval base." Prior to *Rasul,* roughly 700 individuals had been taken into custody at various locations and then transferred to the Guantanamo Bay Naval Station.

More than forty Fellows of the College volunteered to represent detainees, the largest number of lawyers from any one organization to respond to the need for volunteer counsel to represent individuals who were—and remain—not just unpopular, but widely despised by large segments of the population, including, I am sorry to say, many lawyers.

The outpouring of volunteer Fellows was the result of a happy coincidence. The Gibbons Law Firm in Newark, New Jersey, of which Fellow Mike Griffinger is a partner, had sponsored a public interest extern for several years. In 2004–05 that extern, Gita Gutierrez, was working at the Center for Constitutional Rights ("CCR"), one of the first public interest organizations to take up the cause of the Guantanamo detainees. Mike Griffinger learned of the detainee need for counsel from Gita Gutierrez and brought it to the attention of the College's Access to Justice Committee, of which he was a member. That committee approved the concept of encouraging Fellows to represent detainees; the committee's recommendation was enthusiastically endorsed by regent Dennis Supplee, who had oversight responsibility for the committee; and the executive committee approved the recommendation in January 2005 in a specially arranged conference call.

The response from the ranks of Fellows was extraordinary: at last count in 2009, forty-two Fellows had volunteered to act as habeas counsel. They came from all over the country—from Honolulu to Boston and from Portland, Oregon, to Jacksonville Beach, Florida. My personal hero among this cadre is Ed Burke, a Fellow in Honolulu who at the time was, I believe, in his seventies. In order to meet with his detainee client, Ed had to travel from Honolulu to Fort Lauderdale (with at least one connection) and thence by prop plane to Guantanamo. The trip must have taken the better part of two days each way.

Most of the foregoing representations were facilitated by CCR but were undertaken by the Fellows in their own names or in the names of their firms. The College was not identified with the individual volunteering Fellows; no action was taken nor any public statements made by the College—at least until November 2005, when I learned that Senator Lindsay Graham had offered an amendment to the National Defense Authorization Act that would have stripped the federal courts of jurisdiction to entertain a habeas petition by a Guantanamo detainee, in effect nullifying the Supreme Court's decisions in *Rasul, supra,* and *Boumedienne v. Bush.* (In the latter case, the Supreme Court held that Guantanamo detainees are entitled to invoke the constitutional right of habeas corpus.)

I became aware of Senator Graham's proposed amendment on a Friday while visiting my son Jeff in Indiana. I was told that the Senate would vote on the amendment the following Monday. I returned to New York and spent most of the next two days finding the proposed amendment language, pondering what action would be appropriate for the College to take, and gathering the Executive Committee by e-mail and phone. The Executive Committee approved my recommendation that the College should go on record, in the form of a letter addressed individually to each senator, opposing the proposed amendment. I drafted such a letter, which decried the Graham amendment because it "undermine[d] our treasured rule of law." The letter was delivered the following Monday to each member of the Senate before the anticipated vote. Whether or not the letter influenced the outcome, the Graham amendment was defeated.

The College has had a long history of avoiding controversial issues that might be considered "political" and as to which there might be widespread disagreement among the Fellows. Although it was clear to me that preservation of the right to seek a writ of habeas corpus was at its core an issue not of politics, but of constitutional law having transcendent importance, I would have preferred, had time allowed, to consult the members of the board of regents and the past presidents before sending the letter. But time did not allow.

The fall of 2009 seemed an appropriate time to conduct a survey of the forty-two volunteer detainee counsel whom we had identified as college Fellows. They collectively represented eighty-four detainees, who came from twenty different countries. At least thirty-one of the eighty-four had been repatriated to their home countries, and eleven had been resettled elsewhere.

Each of the representations had its own story. At one extreme, the Uzbek client of College past president Mike Mone and his son and partner, Michael, was given refuge in Ireland, where he was reunited with his family. (I do not think it hurt that Mike Mone knows Mary Robinson, former President of Ireland and former UN High Commissioner for Human Rights.) At the other extreme, the representation by Charlotte, North Carolina Fellows George Daly and Jeff Davis of Mane Shaman al-Habardi ended when al-Habardi committed suicide.

Most of the detainees represented by Fellows are unknown to the world beyond their families. Their names will probably die when they do. But at least three will have their places in the history of constitutional law. One is Lakhdar Boumedienne, represented by Fellow Seth Waxman of Washington, D.C.; the *Boumedienne* decision is noted above. On remand from the Supreme Court, Boumedienne's counsel persuaded the District Court to grant their client's habeas petition, and at last report he was living in France as a free man.

Another detainee, Salim Ahmed Hamdan, was represented by Fellow Harry Schneider of Seattle. On Hamdan's petition for certiorari, the Supreme Court held in 2006 that the then-existing military commission procedure had not been authorized by Congress and violated both Common Article Three of the Geneva Conventions and the United States Code of Military Justice. In response to the decision, Congress enacted the Military Commissions Act of 2006, under which Hamdan was the first detainee to be tried. After a three-week trial, Hamdan was convicted, but was sentenced by a military jury to serve only an additional five months.

The third detainee whose story is widely known is Omar Khadr, a Canadian citizen represented by Fellow Barry Coburn of Washington, D.C. Khadr was charged with having murdered an American serviceman when Khadr was fifteen. He eventually pleaded guilty under an agreement providing for his eventual return to Canada. He was repatriated to that country in 2012.

I am inexpressibly proud of the College Fellows who responded to this call for volunteers in the finest tradition of the Bar. In the presidency of Joan Lukey, each of the volunteer Fellows received a plaque expressing the College's appreciation and respect. Each also has the knowledge and satisfaction of having stepped forward to represent the least regarded individuals under our government's control.

28

NEW YORK LAWYER ASSISTANCE TRUST

More than a decade ago, a lawyer and close friend died in his fifties of a heart attack. He had consumed alcohol in large quantities for many years, and I was—and remain—convinced that alcohol contributed to his untimely passing. I have known other lawyers who have consumed alcohol in excess, and I must confess that on occasion I have overindulged and now normally limit myself to one drink of single malt and one or two glasses of wine at dinner.

The practice of law, including but not limited to the craft of advocacy, is highly demanding and stressful, and many lawyers find that alcohol helps them to cope with the demands and stress. There are few studies of the subject of which I am aware, but I have seen at least two that have placed the percentage of lawyers who abuse or are dependent upon alcohol at 15–20 percent, a significantly higher percentage than in the population at large. (I have deliberately differentiated between "alcohol abuse" and "alcohol dependency." Alcohol abuse is excessive drinking at one time or over time. Chronic alcohol abuse can lead to alcohol dependency, which is an addictive illness.)

As I have already mentioned, I created a staff position to address this subject when I was President of the New York City Bar Association. After I stepped down from that positon in 2002, I ceased to have an "official" interest in the subject until August 2007, when I agreed to become Chair of the New York Lawyer Assistance Trust beginning January 1, 2008.

Both the New York State Bar Association and various county bar associations have committees, often called

Lawyer Helping Lawyer Committees, that assist lawyers with alcohol-related issues, but there was no separate statewide body devoted solely to the subject until 2001 after a panel known as the Bellacosa Commission (named after its chair, St. Johns Law School Dean and former Court of Appeals Judge Joseph Bellacosa) recommended the creation of a program to address substance abuse issues with separately designated resources, to be called the Lawyer Assistance Trust (the "Trust"). To emphasize the importance of the Trust, the immediate past president of the New York State Bar Association, James Moore, was appointed in 2001 by Chief Judge Judith Kaye as the first chair of the twenty-one-member board of trustees.

Barbara Smith, longtime counsel to the New York State Ethics Commission, who apparently was looking for a new challenge, became the first executive director. I cannot speak highly enough of Barbara Smith. In a very quiet, self-effacing way, Barbara discharged the duties of her position single-handedly until after a few years she found the funds to hire an assistant. Barbara worked closely with Pat Spataro, her counterpart at the New York State Bar Association; Eileen Travis at the New York City Bar Association; and the individuals holding comparable positions at the relatively few county bar associations (most notably, in my memory, the Erie and Suffolk County Bar Associations) that had similar programs, as well as the American Bar Association, where she was one of ten members of the Commission on Lawyer Assistance Programs and co-chaired a national conference on the subject. Barbara Smith was devoid of ego; she never promoted herself; she was the epitome of the dedicated public servant. She also became a cherished friend.

A brief anecdote speaks volumes about Barbara and our relationship. During my term as president, the Trust met in

New York City from time to time. On one occasion Barbara was unable to return home after the meeting to the Albany suburb in which she lived. I invited her to spend the night with us. In gratitude Barbara gave Nan and me a first edition of John Steinbeck's *Travels with Charley*. The "Charley" in the title was Steinbeck's black standard poodle, after whom Nan and I named our dog of the same breed. Our Charley had taken a shine to Barbara (as he does to most women). The book is prominently displayed in the living room of our Manhattan apartment.

After three years it became apparent that roughly one-third of the inquiries received by the Trust and the New York State and New York City Bar Association programs related principally not to alcohol or drug abuse or dependency, but to depression and other mental health issues. Chief Judge Kaye was persuaded to have the New York Court of Appeals amend the charter of the Trust to broaden its charge to encompass mental health issues, a very welcome change given the much greater prevalence of depression among lawyers (reported by one study to be 19 percent) than in the general population (6.7 percent according to the same study).

Alcohol and other substance abuse and dependency are not confined to practicing lawyers, but extend to members of the judiciary as well. A sixteen-member Judge Advisory Panel was created to provide guidance to the Trust as it addressed outreach, education, and policy changes relating to this aspect of the problem. Judge John C. Rowley of Tompkins County chaired the Judge Advisory Panel energetically and capably.

Jim Moore was succeeded as Chair of the Trust after three years by Dave Pfalzgraf of Buffalo, and in August 2007 I was asked and agreed to succeed Dave for a three-year term beginning January 1, 2008. The board which I joined was a collaborative group. Many were themselves in recovery. (I had not theretofore been aware that a "recovering" alcoholic remains "in recovery" until he or she dies. The personal struggle against relapse is never-ending.) Other board members were treating psychologists or were concerned with related subjects such as the lawyer disciplinary process and the Appellate Division character and fitness committees. I truly looked forward to board meetings, because all of the members were plainly and deeply devoted to a common mission, which they pursued with dedication.

The Trust periodically sponsored a gathering of law school student affairs professionals and mailed at year-end to the roughly 40,000 attorneys in solo or small firm practice throughout the state a brief newsletter and calendar card containing information about the lawyer-assistance services available. A flyer describing the Trust and its activities was given to each lawyer upon admission to the bar. The Trust's law school and pre-law school outreach efforts were headed by Trustee Marjorie Silver, Professor of Law at Touro Law Center, whose dedication and perseverance led to her being honored by the ABA Commission on Lawyer Assistance Programs. Because so many disciplinary matters have their roots in alcoholism, other substance abuse, and mental health problems, the disciplinary authorities were represented on the Trust board in the person of Bob Guido, Nassau County Bar Association Special Counsel for Disciplinary Matters.

An effort was undertaken to adopt a program of conditional admission to the bar, that is, admission conditioned on participation in a recovery program for a stated period of time. While other states had adopted such a program, the effort sadly failed in New York.

A separate and successful effort was made to amend then Disciplinary Rule 1-103 (now Rule 8.3 of the New York

Rules of Professional Conduct) and adopt a new Section 499 of the Judiciary Law to ensure the confidentiality of communications between lawyer assistance program professionals and lawyers seeking their help.

The Trust was funded through attorney licensing fees and had a modest budget. (I cannot recall the precise amount but am relatively confident that it was less $1 million.) In 2010 the Trust gave $242,000 in grants to the New York State and New York City Bar Associations, five county and other city bar associations, and Touro Law School—principally to fund continuing legal education programs.

My three-year term as chair of the Trust ended at December 31, 2010, at which time I was succeeded by Justice Vincent J. Reilly, Jr. I was stunned to learn a few months later that no appropriation had been made for the Trust in the judiciary budget for 2011 (perhaps on the theory that the New York State and New York City Bar Association programs were sufficient to deal with the problem). If the subject were not so serious, I would be tempted to dismiss the defunding decision as "penny wise and pound foolish." As of May 5, 2011, the Trust closed its doors, leaving me with a feeling of deep regret.

I have often looked back wistfully on my positions as Trustee of the New York Lawyers Assistance Trust for six years and Chair for three. I do not know how many lawyers and law students sought and received assistance from the Trust, but whatever the number, the importance of its work during its decade of existence cannot be overstated.

PART V: PRO BONO SERVICE

For more than four decades, I have devoted a significant portion of my time to pro bono work. I have not attempted to add up the hours, but am quite confident that they number in the many thousands. Why have I done so? I was never able to articulate my motivation until I read remarks by Attorney General Loretta Lynch on receiving an award from the Federal Bar Council. "Service," she said, "is the rent we pay for living here on this earth." Pro bono work is one of the most widely available and satisfying ways for lawyers to render service and pay that rent.

I am by no means the only Sullivan & Cromwell lawyer who has felt a personal and professional obligation to engage in pro bono work. I was, however, the first partner in the firm to be asked to oversee the pro bono work of our lawyers. During the years of my oversight responsibilities, many lawyers in the firm volunteered for a wide array of pro bono assignments, ranging from death penalty work (I can recall four such cases) to poverty law, housing, immigration, asylum, disaster relief and civil rights..

A number of Sullivan & Cromwell associates have left the firm to found or lead (or both) organizations that serve the disadvantaged; some of those organizations have become well known. Bob Hayes as a young lawyer founded the Coalition for the Homeless, the first pro bono organization in New York City to devote its work to the all too many homeless persons in our city. Nadine Strossen, with whom I tried a case for Hewlett-Packard in 1980, became the President of the American Civil Liberties Union, a position which she held with distinction for more than a decade. Maria Foscarinis moved to Washington, D.C., where she started the National Center on Homelessness and Poverty, which advocates for the homeless in the halls of government. I am very proud to have known and worked with all of them. They have added luster to the reputation of Sullivan & Cromwell.

The following are some of the more important pro bono and public service assignments I have undertaken individually.

29

THE LEGAL AID SOCIETY

My first contact with the pro bono community occurred when I was asked forty-two years ago to represent the Legal Aid Society, which had been sued by a former client, Noman Thomas. The Society had represented Thomas when he was charged with raping a woman on a rooftop. At the time, the Society's Criminal Defense Division was not organized, as it is now, to provide "vertical representation," that is, the assignment of one lawyer to represent a client from arraignment through trial. Instead, Thomas had a series of lawyers: one for arraignment, another for motions, yet another for trial. The sequential assignments were not conducive to effective coordination, but more importantly trial counsel did not always have an adequate investigative record or the time to fill in the holes.

In this instance, the lawyer assigned by Legal Aid to represent Thomas at trial met with him only once for thirty minutes shortly before trial and contacted none of the potential defense witnesses whose names Thomas had given him. At trial, Thomas himself was the only witness called by his Legal Aid lawyer. Thomas was convicted after a one-day non-jury trial and sentenced to a lengthy prison term.

While in prison, Thomas filed a habeas corpus petition in the Southern District of New York. Judge Marvin Frankel, to whom the case was assigned, appointed counsel, who conducted the investigation that Thomas' Legal Aid counsel had failed to conduct. After a hearing, Judge Frankel granted Thomas's habeas petition in an opinion which excoriated the Society for conducting a defense that was "a farce and a mockery of justice."

On release from prison, Thomas sued Legal Aid for malpractice, and the Society sought representation from Judge Peck, who was on its board at the time. He asked me to undertake the representation, and I agreed to do so. The Society did not have a very good case on the merits for the reasons that had been fully detailed in Judge Frankel's opinion, and I did not want to defend the suit by arguing on the Society's behalf that Thomas, its former client, had in fact been guilty. I crafted an argument that the Society ought to have the same immunity from civil suit that was afforded to prosecutors. Unfortunately, the argument had little going for it but symmetry, and it was rejected by the Honorable Louis Fusco of the Supreme Court, Bronx County. The case was settled shortly thereafter.

That representation brought me into contact with the Society's Attorney-in-Chief, Archibald R. Murray, who oversaw all of the Society's divisions: Civil, Criminal, Juvenile Rights, and the Elderly. The Society maintained what I believe was the largest "law office" in the country second only to the United States Department of Justice. Arch Murray was a brilliant lawyer and one of the most decent people I have known, and the attorneys in charge of the Society's divisions were extraordinarily capable leaders in their own right.

In 1977, at the ripe old age of forty-one, I was invited to join the Society's board of directors, and a scant four years later I was elected president. I cannot state as a fact, though I believe, that Arthur Liman, a Paul, Weiss partner and perhaps the most highly regarded commercial trial and appellate advocate in the City, had been the first choice of the Legal Aid board, but Arthur was not available because he was serving as chief counsel to the Senate committee investigating the Iran-Contra Affair. When my two-year term as president of the Society expired, Arthur's service to the Senate committee had ended, and he succeeded me.

Despite my four years of board service (or perhaps because that period had been so relatively brief), I was not well prepared to take leadership of an organization of the scale and complexity of the Legal Aid Society. Fortunately, with Arch Murray and his lieutenants at the helm, I did not have many opportunities to screw up.

The president of the Legal Aid Society had few perquisites, one of which was to select the recipient of the Society's Servant of Justice Award. I selected Judge Peck, who fully deserved the award wholly independently of the fact that we were partners. I drafted the tribute to him for inclusion in the dinner program, and while attending a spring meeting of the American College of Trial Lawyers, I asked Whitney North Seymour if he would look at the draft. I have a vivid memory of sitting with him in his hotel room and watching him mark up the draft in pen. Whitney was elderly and in ill health, but he summoned his energy to polish a fitting tribute for his old friend.

Whitney North Seymour died two years after the dinner honoring Judge Peck. I attended the funeral at Grace Church, of which he had been a congregant for many years. Shortly before the service began, I observed Arthur H. Dean and John J. McCloy, former head of Milbank Tweed and High Commissioner for Germany, entering the church arm in arm. They were followed by Judge Harold Medina, who was wheelchair-bound and in his nineties. I recall having the distinct sense that I was witnessing the passing of a generation of legal giants.

I have one particularly fond memory of my term as president of the Legal Aid Society. The chair of the Legal Aid board was Helen Buttenwieser, the only woman lawyer of her generation I ever met. Helen devoted her life to social causes.

Archibald Murray, David W. Peck, Whitney North Seymour, and MAC (The Legal Aid Society)

She was seventy-six years old when I became president of Legal Aid, but she had the energy of someone half her age. Independently wealthy (she was a scion of the Lehman family), Helen was driven by a chauffeur. In order to make her car easier to spot, she chose one that was painted fire-engine red, and because she was small and thrifty, the car was what we now call a compact. Visualizing Helen being escorted by the chauffeur into her little red car calls to mind the saying: "Only in New York."

30

VOLUNTEERS OF LEGAL SERVICE

When my term as Legal Aid president ended, I sought other opportunities to serve the poor and otherwise disadvantaged with unmet legal needs. Such an opportunity presented itself in the form of Volunteers of Legal Service ("VOLS"), which had been created in 1984 under the umbrella of the New York City Bar Association but was later established as a separate organization with its own board. I was elected to that board in 1996 and have continued to be a member ever since.

The driving force at VOLS from shortly after its inception till a few years ago was William Johnson ("Bill") Dean. Bill is a Renaissance man: he has been a columnist for the *Christian Science Monitor*, a devotee of the New York Society Library and the Century Association, a blogger, and an avid basketball player.

At or shortly after its inception, VOLS had persuaded thirty of the largest New York City law firms to commit to provide thirty hours per lawyer per year of pro bono service. To the best of my knowledge, VOLS' "pledge" was the first quantification in New York of a pro bono commitment. Over the years, VOLS has created separate projects to aid the elderly, children, immigrants, and micro-entrepreneurs (the latter project being the first of its kind in the metropolitan New York area and perhaps in the country).

Three years ago, Bill Dean "retired." As a retirement gift, I arranged to have Bill given a set of basketball lessons by a professional coach who numbers NBA players among his clients. Bill Dean was succeeded by Bill Lienhard, who has brought both energy and vision to VOLS. The organization has not skipped a beat and is more vibrant than ever. VOLS for many years had its offices in the old, ornate building on lower Park Avenue owned by the Federation of Protestant Philanthropies. When the building was sold and VOLS was forced to move when its lease expired in September 2015, I was able, with the generous assistance of friends, to help VOLS find new, more spacious and more attractive quarters at 40 Worth Street.

31

THE VANCE CENTER

Another pro bono organization conceived under the auspices of the New York City Bar Association is the Cyrus R. Vance Center for International Justice, on whose board (called the "Cyrus Vance Committee") I served for two decades before taking emeritus status. Inosi Nyatta and Werner Ahlers, both Sullivan & Cromwell partners, are currently committee members.

The Vance Center traces its origins to a three-day conference the New York City Bar Association convened in April 2000 while I was president. The purpose of the conference, which was attended by representatives from fourteen countries, was to compare approaches taken in those and other countries to addressing the civil legal needs of the poor.

As a direct outgrowth of that conference, I and a few others from the Association were invited in 2001 to make presentations to lawyers at several Buenos Aires law firms. I recall that the turnout at the Marval firm, which we visited first, was surprisingly large. As the day progressed and we moved from firm to firm, the number of lawyers in attendance grew smaller and smaller. I wondered whether word was spreading that what we had to say was not worth listening to. In fact, as I learned at the end of the afternoon, the Argentine peso had completely collapsed that day, and law firms were being besieged by calls from clients.

The following year a small delegation that included Association President Leo Milonas and me was invited to make a similar presentation in Santiago, Chile. Although fewer lawyers attended than had in Buenos Aires, I believe we planted the seeds of a pro bono ethic that has taken root in Chile.

A serendipitous bonus of my Chilean visit was the opportunity to acquire a bronze sculpture by the great Chilean artist Mario Irarrazabal, a former priest who had been imprisoned during the Pinochet regime. He is best known for a 36-foot-tall statue of a human hand rising from the northern Chilean desert at an altitude of 1,100 meters. I have never understood why his hauntingly evocative work is not exhibited and sold in the United States.

Like VOLS, the Vance Center has a relatively new Executive Director, Alex Papachristou, who has reinvigorated the organization. The Vance Center has broadened its focus to address problems in four thematic areas: human rights and access to justice (the original core program), the environment, freedom of expression, and health and development. While its initial efforts were in South America, the Vance Center reach now includes Mexico, Central America, and Africa (in particular, the Central African Republic). In recent years the Vance Center has expanded its efforts to include women in the profession and international human rights, including the International Criminal Court in The Hague. The Center has also continued its South African Legal Fellows program, whose genesis under the auspices of the New York City Bar Association I have already described

Five years ago the Vance Center convened a "summit" to bring together the Central and South American lawyers and others whom it had inspired to devote their time and talents to this area. Another "summit" was convened at the New York City Bar Association not long ago. It fills me with pride to realize that the Vance Center through its international network of lawyers has bettered the lives of an untold number of people in other countries.

32

LAWYERS' COMMITTEE FOR CIVIL RIGHTS UNDER LAW

I have had a strong interest in civil rights work for as long as I can remember, dating back to my secondary school education at Horace Mann School. When I was a young associate during the civil rights protests of 1963 and 1964, I was consumed by the seemingly never-ending demands of the Hudson & Manhattan condemnation case, and did not believe that I could devote time to outside pro bono work of a civil rights nature or any other kind. In fact, the Hudson & Manhattan case was on trial at the time of the March 1965 march from Selma to Montgomery.

By the 1980s, feeling more secure in my position in the firm, I was brought by my partner Bob MacCrate to the attention of the Lawyers' Committee for Civil Rights Under Law, one of the pillars of the civil rights community. The Lawyers' Committee had been organized in 1963 when President Kennedy, at the urging of his brother, Attorney General Robert Kennedy, pointed to the severe underrepresentation of black people in the South and asked rhetorically: "Where are the lawyers?" President Kennedy followed that speech by inviting the leaders of the establishment bar, including Arthur H. Dean and Norris Darrell of Sullivan & Cromwell, to the White House—an invitation that could not be refused—and urged them to encourage and provide representation to blacks in the South.

The Lawyers' Committee was organized following that gathering at the White House and has been a commitment of the private bar ever since. Arthur Dean was one of the early co-chairs. Sometime in the '80s I joined the Lawyers' Committee board. (Two of my partners, Chris Mann and

Tracy High, also currently serve on the board.) The Lawyers' Committee has long had two co-chairs with staggered two-year terms of office. In 1993 I was elected co-chair. During my term of office, we celebrated the 30th anniversary of the founding of the Lawyers' Committee. We were invited to the White House for a celebratory reception, and I had the opportunity to meet President Clinton. A similar White House reception was held on the 50th anniversary of the Lawyers' Committee three years ago.

One of the pleasures of being in the Lawyers' Committee leadership has been the experience of working with its long-time President and Executive Director, Barbara Arnwine, who retired in June 2015. Barbara is truly a force of nature, and when she gets going, Barbara speaks in a rolling cadence that brings to mind Martin Luther King and the other great civil rights leaders. Under Barbara's leadership, the Lawyers' Committee has become a powerful force in the civil rights community. Barbara recently stepped down as president and executive director. I have attended only one board meeting with her successor, Kristin Clarke. If Kristen measures up to the impression she created at that board meeting and to the reports I have heard—and I have no doubt she will—the leadership of the Lawyers' Committee is in good hands.

Combating suppression of the black and other minority vote has been at the core of the Lawyers' Committee's work since its formation. In 2004, the Lawyers' Committee played a prominent role in the "Get Out the Vote" efforts of the civil rights community. Phone banks were set up at law firms, including (I am proud to say) Sullivan & Cromwell's 125 Broad Street office, which individuals who were being rebuffed at the polls could call for telephonic advice using a well-advertised call-in phone number. We had roughly fifty volunteers, including both lawyers and administrative staff,

MAC with President Clinton

at the Sullivan & Cromwell phone bank. They were responsible for fielding inquiries from three states. It is my recollection that by midnight on Election Day, the volunteers at our phone bank had spoken to nearly 3,000 callers who had encountered difficulty voting. We established a similar phone bank in 2008, and in 2012 a training session for phone bank volunteers was conducted at our office.

I have my association with the Lawyers' Committee to thank for the opportunity to work on the South Carolina Voting Rights Act case described above.

33

REENTRY TASK FORCE

In August 2007, Barry Kamins, then-president of the New York City Bar Association, appointed me to chair a newly created Task Force on Employment Opportunities for the Formerly Incarcerated. From personal experience, he knew that it was crucial that those who are released from jail or prison have a chance to make a living wage and develop the economic, social, and psychological underpinnings to lead productive and satisfying lives. Barry believed that law firms could and should set an example by hiring former inmates.

Barry's choice of me as Task Force chair was certainly not based on my qualifications. The subject was one about which I knew next to nothing. My practice had been almost exclusively civil, and even apart from my professional life, I had given little thought to the problems encountered by individuals on being released from incarceration.

The Task Force had a diverse composition, including current and former members of the judiciary, law firm and bar association leaders, and the executives of two workforce intermediaries, nonprofit organizations that were committed to aiding the formerly incarcerated: Mindy Tarlow of the Center for Employment Opportunities and Judy Whiting of the Legal Action Center. Both Mindy and Judy were highly knowledgeable and articulate, and they made major contributions to the work of the Task Force. Another Task Force member was Bill Snipes, an African-American partner of Sullivan & Cromwell, who has been a moving force in the Pipeline Crisis, which mobilizes private sector leadership to create pathways for young black men to achieve social and economic equality.

The Task Force provided an introduction for me to two of the most remarkable citizens of our city: Charles J. ("Joe") Hynes, then District Attorney of Kings County, and George McDonald, the founder of the Doe Fund.

Joe Hynes met regularly with individuals who had just been released on parole in Brooklyn and Queens to encourage the parolees to seek gainful employment and reunite with family members. He spoke to them not as an authority figure but as a public servant and fellow citizen genuinely concerned for their well-being. I attended one of those meetings and was moved by the effort Joe Hynes made to connect with his audience.

George McDonald and the Doe Fund are a New York City legend. George began distributing food to the homeless who frequent Grand Central Terminal while he was running for Congress in the '80s. One of the beneficiaries of his charity was an elderly black woman who came to be known as "Mama" (her given name was unknown) who sat slumped against the wall in the station waiting room. Mama was ejected from the station by the Metro-North police on a freezing Christmas Eve in 1985. Suffering from pneumonia, she was found dead on the sidewalk on Christmas Day.

George McDonald and his wife Harriet, inspired by the plight of Mama Doe, founded the Doe Fund to provide employment training and, if necessary, housing to homeless men and women, most of whom are ex-offenders who have not been able to reunite with a family or find a job after release from prison or jail. I visited the Doe Fund headquarters together with Cyrus Vance, Jr., who was contemplating running for the office of District Attorney of New York County, to which he was subsequently elected. Cy and I were shown the dormitory rooms where the "men in blue" slept, as well as the dining room where they ate food that had been prepared and served by others of their cohort. (The "men in blue" name derives from the color of the uniform worn by the Doe Fund residents who clean up trash on the upper east side of Manhattan.)

The statistical underpinning of the Task Force's work was stark and irrefutable. The United States has the largest prison population in the world, with only 5 percent of the world's population but roughly 25 percent of its prisoners. A study within the past decade reported that one out of every 100 adults in the United States was incarcerated. The starkest statistic to me is that in 2008 (the year our report was issued) every black male child born in the United States had a 1-in-3 chance of serving a prison sentence at some point in his life.[16] More recent studies establish that conditions have not greatly improved to the extent they have improved at all.

The enormity of those numbers appears to be gradually entering the consciousness of the public and, more importantly, the legislators who design and administrators who oversee our federal and state penal systems. In his valedictory address on September 23, 2014, United States Attorney General Eric Holder announced with pride that for the first time in twenty-four years, the federal prison population had fallen rather than risen. The federal Sentencing Commission has adjusted downward the scoring system for sentencing drug offenders, and just a few months ago 6,000 federal prisoners were ordered to be released earlier than had been expected.

Our country's incarceration policies have long imposed an immense cost, both social and economic: it has been estimated that the annual cost of maintaining a prisoner in New

---

[16] *One in 100: Behind Bars in the United States*, The Pew Center on the States (Feb. 2008).

York State prisons is $42,000; the comparable figure for New York City jails is more than $60,000.[17] According to a 2006 report by the Independent Commission on Reentry and Employment, each year in New York State alone 127,000 individuals were released from prisons and jails. When they seek employment, they encounter many obstacles: they lack the skills required for many positions and do not have the contacts to social networks through which jobs may be found. They are barred from many employment opportunities by statute and cannot obtain licenses that are granted only to those of "good moral character." Although certificates of relief from disabilities and certificates of good conduct may be issued by parole boards (the former may also be granted by the sentencing court), certificate applications may take as long as eighteen months to process.

I can personally testify that there is a widespread prejudice against former inmates based on irrational fear. Our Task Force sent a survey to the human resources directors at large New York City law firms and received eleven responses. Four of the eleven stated that they would be reluctant to hire an ex-offender because of trust/honesty and/or safety concerns—regardless of the nature of the crime committed by the individual.

In March 2008, only seven months after its creation, the Task Force issued its report, "Legal Employers Taking the Lead: Enhancing Employment Opportunities for the Previously Incarcerated." The report both described the enormity of the problem and sought to allay fears about employing the formerly incarcerated. I sent a copy to the human resources directors of the leading New York City law firms, and Barry

---

[17] *Public Safety, Public Spending: Forecasting America's Prison Population*, The Pew Charitable Trusts (Jan. 2007).

Kamins sent one to the managing partners of the thirty largest firms and featured the report in his column in the Association newsletter. The New York City Bar Association proceeded to appoint a director for a newly created Reentry Law Project.

Unfortunately, I cannot point to any hard evidence that our effort otherwise bore fruit. In the end, if I ask myself whether the time and energy I put into this project over seven months was worth the effort and would I expend it again knowing the outcome, the answer is unqualifiedly "yes." The problem of reintegrating the formerly incarcerated into society is real; it has immense ramifications in both human and dollar cost; and it will not go away without sustained effort. Fortunately, Governor Cuomo appreciates the enormity and severity of the problem and has formed a Council on Community Reentry and Reintegration to "address obstacles formerly incarcerated people face upon re-entering society." In announcing the Council's formation, Governor Cuomo expressed his determination "to stop the revolving door of recidivism." I fervently hope that he achieves that goal.

34

FUNDING CIVIL LEGAL SERVICES

In the fall of 1997, prompted by a report by a New York Assembly committee calling for an appropriation of $40 million to fund civil legal services programs, Chief Judge Judith Kaye created the Civil Legal Services Project to "determine how society can best support legal services" and to find a way of "promot[ing] constancy in the flow of resources for professional legal services organizations." She invited me to become chair and appointed twenty-one individuals to serve on the Project, including private practitioners, corporate counsel, individuals from the industrial and financial services sectors, and representatives of legal services programs. Two senior employees of the Office of Court Administration, Antonio Galvao and Barbara Mulé, functioned as project staff, providing helpful statistical and other information. A third-year law student at New York University Law School, Jeff Chapman, who upon graduation became an associate of Sullivan & Cromwell, also assisted our research.

There was a wealth of information—studies, surveys, and reports—on the subject, but we nevertheless solicited information and views from all legal services providers and bar associations throughout the state. As chair, I met with Chief Judge Kaye and then with Chief Administrative Judge (and later Chief Judge) Jonathan Lippman.

The data we gathered was disturbing, to put it mildly. Between 1990 and 1995 the number of New Yorkers living below 125 percent of the poverty level—the benchmark used by many legal services providers as a qualification for assistance—had increased from 3.4 million to 3.9 million, while the average income of the poorest families in New York had decreased by 20 percent. The effects of these conditions took a terrible toll on the poorest among us. Nine out of ten tenants in summary eviction proceedings lacked counsel. The needs were numerous, varied and severe: income maintenance (including food stamps, unemployment benefits, social security and SSI), debt collection and wage garnishment, family violence, and the list goes on.

At the same time that these pressing needs continued and worsened, the funding for civil legal services was dwindling. In 1998, the two principal sources of that funding—federal Legal Services Corporation grants and the IOLA Fund[18]—were generating $40 million less on an inflation-adjusted basis than they had six years earlier. The resulting squeeze caused legal services providers to reduce staff and shorten their hours of intake. One project member, an upstate businessman named Lewis Golub, reported being stunned when the local legal services provider he visited closed its intake window each day at 10 a.m, only an hour or so after the window had opened. He had not previously known of the problem, but became a dedicated supporter of the project after that experience.

We considered several sources of additional funding for civil legal services: (1) an increase in the filing fees for all courts of general and limited jurisdiction; (2) acceleration of the date for payment of filing fees and attorney registration fees; (3) imposing a fee on entry of a judgment; (4) allocation of a portion of a punitive damages award; (5) allocation of a portion of pre- and post-judgment interest; (6) creation

[18] IOLA (the acronym for "interest on lawyers' accounts") is a mechanism for aggregating funds that clients leave with their lawyers in escrow that are too small or held too briefly to generate income net of associated costs. These deposits are aggregated, and the interest earned on the funds paid over to the IOLA Board, which makes grants to legal services providers.

of a fund consisting of interest on broker accounts (amounts paid in escrow to real estate agents); (7) allocation of a portion of unclaimed class-action proceeds; and (8) allocation of a portion of moneys paid into the Abandoned Property Fund—sometimes referred to as "escheated" funds.

In considering these alternative potential funding sources, we focused on their amount, stability from year to year, and permanency. In the end, we decided to recommend an allocation from the annual increments to the Abandoned Property Fund. Few people are aware that unclaimed interest, dividends, and insurance proceeds totaled almost $300 million a year in New York State alone at the time of our study. Not only was the amount sizable, it was stable year-to-year. While the owners of previously escheated property might lay claim thereto at any time because such claims are not subject to a statute of limitations, the net increase to the fund predictably exceeded $200 million a year. The excess of the amount in the Abandoned Property Fund over the amount required, in the Comptroller's discretion, to satisfy claims against the fund was paid into the General Fund of the State.

We drafted legislation to implement our recommendation that $25 million be allocated each year from the Abandoned Property Fund to fund civil legal services, and I took the train to Albany to present our proposal. I met first with Jim Maguire, counsel to the Governor, who after listening attentively suggested I speak to the leaders of the Legislature. I then met with the counsel to Senate Majority Leader Joseph Bruno, who having also listened attentively recommended that I present our proposal to the Speaker of the Assembly, Sheldon Silver. The Speaker gave me the same courteous audience and, at the end, said that I should speak to the Governor's counsel.

It did not take me long to realize that I was being given

the old run-around. That realization did not assuage my disappointment, but it did disillusion me about the legislative process in New York State, and that disillusionment has remained with me to this day and been reinforced by the recent criminal convictions of the two principal legislative leaders. We nonetheless presented our report and recommendation in May 1998 to Chief Judge Kaye. I am proud of the work our task force accomplished over eight months, and I continue to believe that our recommendation—an annual allotment of $25 million from the Abandoned Property Fund—had irrefutable support in the factual record.

35

PRO BONO NET

The "justice gap," as it has become known, has been with us for decades, and it has only widened over the years. State funding of civil legal services has been paltry, and I have permanent scars from my one unsuccessful attempt (described above) to increase the funding from Albany. The federal Legal Services Corporation is a laudable organization (Harvard Law School Dean Martha Minow, one of my heroes in legal education, is the Vice-Chair), but it must struggle annually for its congressional appropriation, which has never been generous. And while the legal community is supportive of legal services programs, the image that comes to mind is of a boy with his finger in the dike.

So I was more than ordinarily curious when, not long after I stepped down as President of the New York City Bar Association, a young Latham & Watkins partner, Michael Hertz, asked whether I would have lunch with him and Mark O'Brien, the Davis Polk pro bono coordinator, to discuss an organization they were forming to use technology to facilitate the connection between the poor and disadvantaged, on the one hand, and the legal services providers and volunteer lawyers who could help them, on the other. Though I am an incorrigible Luddite (I have yet to master the iPad that Nan gave me), I instinctively felt that Michael and Mark had the germ of a very powerful idea: that if there was a growing gap between the need for legal services and the resources available to meet that need, technology might enable the need and resources to connect more efficiently.

At or shortly after that lunch, Michael and Mark asked if I would become the founding board chair of Pro Bono

Net, and I agreed. We gradually formed a board of directors, anchored by Michael Mills, then chief technology officer at Davis, Polk, and Bill Pollak, then chief executive officer of American Lawyer Media. The relationship with The American Lawyer has been very helpful to Pro Bono Net throughout its existence and was vital in the organization's early years. I recruited to the board Jack Londen, a Morrison & Foerster partner in San Francisco, whom I had come to know and admire through the Lawyers' Committee for Civil Rights Under Law, and Alan Greer, a Miami trial and appellate lawyer, whom I had known since we were adversaries in the Ecological Science Corporation litigation described above. Dave Heiner, a litigation associate at Sullivan & Cromwell many years ago who left the firm to join our client, Microsoft, where he has risen to the position of Vice President and Deputy General Counsel, joined the board in or about 2008, a wonderful addition with whom I was delighted to reunite.

The initial eponymous program created by Pro Bono Net enabled lawyers to register without charge to gain access to a website on which they could find both legal services providers seeking volunteers and also training materials in areas of the law with which the volunteers were not familiar. The site was an instant success because it met the need felt by associates in large law firms for an efficient way to find pro bono clients. Pro Bono Net now has more than 100,000 members, and in the first half of 2014 there were nearly three million visits to PBN sites in more than twenty states in which well over half of the nation's families in poverty live, ranging from Minnesota to Texas and Florida, and from New York and North Carolina to California and Washington.

After 9/11, there was an instant dramatically large demand for legal assistance from victims and their families. Working with The Legal Aid Society, the New York City

Bar Association and others, Pro Bono Net created a disaster site, which more than 2,000 New York City area lawyers visited. Four years later, after Hurricane Katrina wreaked havoc in southern Louisiana and adjacent states, Pro Bono Net, working with bar associations in Louisiana and Mississippi, created a similar disaster site, as it did after the tornadoes that devastated the lower Midwest some years ago and again after Sandy flooded large portions of the metropolitan New York City area in October 2012. Drawing on these experiences, Pro Bono Net has created a National Disaster Legal Aid Resource Center, a centralized resource on legal issues related to all types of disasters, to recruit and mobilize pro bono attorneys in the aftermath of a disaster, and to provide accurate and timely information on disaster-related legal issues to low- and moderate-income people.

Having responded to the demand by lawyers for opportunities, Pro Bono Net turned to the other half of the equation by creating, in partnership with legal services organizations, LawHelp, an Internet site that provides low- and moderate-income people with free, online information about legal aid programs in their communities, answers to questions about their legal rights, court information, and links to social service agencies. LawHelp has launched a Spanish-only website in Puerto Rico. In New York, Pro Bono Net has worked with the court system to support the e-filing of domestic offense petitions in all sixty-two counties.

Has LawHelp been a success? I would say so, judging by its nearly 7.6 million visits in the first ten months of 2015. In a natural progression, Pro Bono Net has created a mobile platform in several states that provides legal information and referrals on consumer debt, domestic violence, and driver's license reinstatement issues.

Pro Bono Net then took a leap to create LawHelpInteractive,

which allows low-income people to prepare their own legal forms without charge in areas like consumer debt, eviction, and child custody and support. LawHelpInteractive is still in its early years, but it has attracted considerable online traffic, with nearly one million client interviews and more than 500,000 document assemblies in 2014. LawHelpInteractive is now operational in forty-three states and territories

Pro Bono Net has also created more than twenty "national" issue sites, of which the most widely visited is the Immigration Advocates Network, which has nearly 7,800 members and has had more than 360,000 visits in 2015. Other national sites include CitizenshipWorks, Reentry Net, a domestic violence site, a wage-and-hour clearinghouse, and the ABA Military Pro Bono Project. When I look at the metrics of the usage of the various Pro Bono Net sites, I am truly in awe of the contribution Pro Bono Net has made to responding to the needs of so many of our citizens and non-citizen residents. With support from the New York State Office of Victim Services, Pro Bono Net has just begun development of a Crime Victims' Legal Network. Pro Bono Net has increased the size of its small staff to assist in administering all these programs.

In 2013 the Legal Services Corporation convened a summit on the use of technology to expand access to justice. That summit found that the multiple websites providing information on court, legal services, and private bar resources were confusing and recommended that every state have a single access to justice portal so that information will be available anywhere and anytime to anyone seeking assistance. The National Center for State Courts has developed the requirements of such a portal. Pro Bono Net is working with Microsoft to create the portal.

During its first fifteen years, there have been leadership

changes at Pro Bono Net. Michael Hertz left to become a partner at White & Case, but has remained a staunch board member. Mark O'Brien now wears the hats of both CEO and COO. He has a strong supporting cast. When Bill Pollak, who had succeeded me as board chair in 2010 and performed splendidly in that position, stepped down in June of last year, Dave Heiner succeeded Bill. I could not have been more pleased.

By any measure of productivity, Pro Bono Net is a remarkable organization. I marvel at what has grown from the germ of an idea that Michael Hertz and Mark O'Brien presented to me at lunch fifteen years ago. I have watched Pro Bono grow from infancy to adulthood and am immensely proud of what it has accomplished and still aspires and strives to do.

36

MY LONGEST AND FINAL REPRESENTATION

As I was encouraging other Fellows of the American College of Trial Lawyers to volunteer to represent detainees at Guantanamo Bay, I quickly realized that I should put my money where my mouth was, so to speak, and contacted the Center for Constitutional Rights to identify an individual detainee in need of a lawyer.

Undertaking the Representation

CCR gave me the names of four detainees, who had been identified by Moazzam Begg, a former detainee and British citizen who had been repatriated not long before. One of those four was Adel El-Ouerghi (sometimes spelled "Al-Wirghi"), a Tunisian by birth, for whose family in Tunis CCR had both a home address and a phone number. We enlisted a Tunisian human rights lawyer, Bochra Hmida, to contact the family. Although the phone number and address we gave Bochra proved to be incorrect, she was nevertheless somehow able to find the family.

We proceeded to draft a habeas petition, drawing upon others previously filed on behalf of detainees, and filed the petition in the United States District Court for the District of Columbia on July 29, 2005. Moazzam Begg agreed to sign the petition as a "next friend," as we could not yet secure Adel's signature. The case was assigned to Chief Judge Lamberth. Our next step was to seek security clearance in order that we might visit Adel. That process took almost six months and included an interview by a retired FBI agent. After receiving clearance, I proceeded to retain an interpreter (who also had obtained clearance) and make travel arrangements.

Guantanamo

In 2005 detainee counsel could reach Guantanamo by only one route. They had to fly first to Fort Lauderdale and then take an extremely noisy and unbelievably slow prop plane owned by a government contract airline. At the time of my first trip, there were two such carriers, Lynx and Air Sunshine. Air Sunshine was so unreliable that it earned the nickname "Air Sometime." It was reputed to have the worst safety record of all airlines subject to regulation by the FAA. The trip took three to three-and-a-half hours due to the aging aircraft, the necessity of detouring to avoid Cuban airspace, and perhaps a desire to conserve fuel and thereby save money. The prospect of flying for that length of time in a plane with no bathroom terrified me, and I don't use that word lightly. On my first trip, I brought a bottle and a raincoat for privacy in case my bladder failed me. On later trips, I learned to reduce my intake of liquids for the twenty-four hours preceding a flight. Fortunately, I never had a mishap.

Visiting counsel were put up at the former military Combined Bachelor Quarters ("CBQ"). The accommodations consisted of not uncomfortable two-room suites, each with a bathroom and tiny kitchenette. The incoming Lynx Air flight arrived between 5 and 6 p.m. By the time one had baggage searched and took the bus from the airstrip to the CBQ, the sole nearby cafeteria had closed, leaving available only pizza and buffalo wings at the adjacent bar. Necessity being the mother of invention, a nice tradition arose. At the end of an interview day, on the way back to the CBQ counsel would purchase food at the commissary for themselves and also for counsel who were arriving that afternoon; both groups would eat dinner together at a communal outdoor grill. That friendly gesture fostered a feeling of comradery among individuals who in most cases had not previously known each other but shared a common mission.

The routine of visits to detainees never varied. One took a bus or walked the approximately two miles from the CBQ to the ferry dock on the leeward side of Guantanamo Bay for the 8 a.m. ferry, which took about twenty minutes to reach the dock on the windward side. There counsel were met by a military escort. After being given identification badges, counsel were bussed to the interview site, which was never identified in advance. On the way, the bus would stop at a shopping center containing a Subway fast-food restaurant, where a lawyer could buy eggs, toast, or a muffin and coffee to bring to one's client.

The physical layout of the detention camps (translate "prisons"), including the rooms where counsel interviewed their clients, is classified information. I believe I can say, however, that the interview settings were cramped, and I always assumed the interviews were both videotaped and recorded. Around 11:30 a.m. there was a lunch break during which the detainees prayed and counsel were taken by bus to the Subway restaurant, where we bought food both for ourselves and to take back to our clients, with whom we shared the midday meal. Sometime around 4 p.m. there was a rap on the door to tell us the interview day was ending. We returned to the ferry dock for the trip back to the CBQ.

I took several trips to Guantanamo. Illness prevented me from joining my colleague Jessica Klein on the last two trips. Of the trips I took, two stand out in my mind. One was the first trip, on which I was accompanied by Suhana Han, then an associate and now a partner at Sullivan & Cromwell. When we entered the interview room, Adel shook my hand but demurred, because of his Muslim faith, at touching Suhana, a woman. He excused himself graciously. After preliminaries, I told Adel that I was Jewish and asked whether he was willing to be represented by a Jewish lawyer. He half-smiled and replied that many of the "brothers" had Jewish lawyers and that Jews and Muslims have common ancestors according to the Bible.

At the outset of a later visit, when the bus transporting us reached the compound where the interview was to take place, I was informed by an officer that Adel did not wish to see me. After having represented Adel for a few years and just traveled for two days to meet with him, I was stunned. I hastily drafted a letter asking that Adel change his mind, had the letter translated, and gave it to the officer to deliver. He returned some minutes later to say that Adel would in fact see me, and the interview proceeded. Though I don't know for a fact what had happened, I strongly suspect that one of the guards had poked Adel while he was sleeping to tell him that we had arrived, and Adel, still half-asleep, had told the guard to leave him alone and turned over in his bed to go back to sleep.

Over the course of my visits I came to have a sense of Adel as a person. Though uneducated, he was intelligent, quick-witted, and had a sense of humor as well as irony. I fully believe that these qualities enabled him to survive his twelve-and-a-half years at Guantanamo without losing his mind or developing a hatred for anyone and anything American. He also was curious about the world outside Guantanamo. I told him about my family and added that I owned and rode a horse, a Clydesdale/Morgan mix named Marcel, which particularly interested him.

Our habeas petition and others were effectively placed on hold till the *Boumedienne* case was decided by the Supreme Court. When the deeply divided Court held that detainees were entitled to seek habeas relief, we considered how to proceed. I cannot disclose client confidences, but can say that based on all of the information we had accumulated from various sources, I concluded that our chances of obtaining relief would be greatly improved if we could locate and obtain testimony, if necessary via videotaped deposition, from Adel's wife, Kadija, whom he had married a couple of years before he was taken into custody.

We had no address or phone number for Kadija, but miraculously made contact with her at an International Red Cross office in or near Kandahar in southeastern Afghanistan near the border with Pakistan. Kadija was highly emotional during our phone conversation, which made it difficult to gather information and discuss a proposed course of action. We did learn, however, that she wanted to join Adel's family in Tunisia, but the Tunisian government had denied her visa application. Our conversation ended inconclusively. After a few more years, during which we were unable to contact her, Kadija lost all hope of being reunited with Adel, secured a divorce, and remarried. I do not know to this day how Adel coped with this devastating news.

In the first nine years of Adel's imprisonment, Tunisia was a dictatorship ruled by the iron fist of President Zine Al-Abidine Ben Ali. In or about 2003 the Tunisian government passed an anti-terrorism law and then proceeded to charge and convict Adel (and other Guantanamo detainees) in absentia and without notice. Adel was sentenced to a twenty-year prison term. We tried through Bochra Hmida to obtain a copy of the judgment of conviction but were unable to do so. We filed a motion to enjoin our government from transferring Adel to Tunisia. The motion was granted. As matters turned out, this was the only judicial relief we ever obtained for Adel.

False Hope

Then in January 2011 came the "Arab Spring," which in fact began with the overthrow of the Ben Ali regime in Tunisia and soon spread to Egypt. A "democratic" government was formed in Tunisia, and the following year representatives of that government went to Guantanamo to visit their imprisoned countrymen and then proceeded to Washington to meet with Ambassador Daniel Fried, who had been tasked by the Obama Administration with arranging for the repatriation or resettlement of those detainees who were considered suitable candidates if appropriate arrangements could be made. Adel was deemed such a candidate after the interagency review of each detainee's situation ordered by President Obama immediately after taking office. (Indeed, Adel had reportedly been cleared for transfer by the Bush Administration in 2008, though we did not know it at the time.)

I met with the Tunisian Permanent Representative to the UN in New York City and then in Washington, D.C., with Hedi Ben Abbess, a member of the Tunisian delegation who was to meet the following day with Ambassador Fried. Ben Abbess, who was the Tunisian Assistant Secretary of State for the Americas and who spoke English perfectly, informed me that his government was most eager to receive the Tunisians at Guantanamo and that he had brought with him formal declarations from several Tunisian ministries of their willingness and readiness to receive their detained countrymen.

I had great hopes that Adel would finally return home a free man until the Tunisian government in which Ben Abbess served collapsed. I do not know whether the successor government, which was reported by the press to be headed by a moderate Islamic group, continued to press for the return of the Tunisian detainees, but if it did, I doubt that the U.S. government would have considered it an acceptable location for resettlement.

In any event, Congress effectively put an end to transfers from Guantanamo by inserting in the National Defense Reauthorization Act in 2011 a provision prohibiting the transfer of detainees unless the Secretary of Defense "certified" in writing as a fact that the government of the country to which the detainee was to be transferred "has taken, or agreed to take effective actions to ensure that the individual cannot take action to threaten the United States...." The same provision was included in the 2012 and 2013 enactments. It would have required extraordinary courage—some would say foolhardiness—for Secretary of Defense Panetta to vouch for actions taken or to be taken by a foreign government, and in fact he signed no certificates while those statutes were in effect.

The 2014 Reauthorization Act made a subtle change: instead of requiring the Secretary of Defense to certify to facts over which he had no control, the Secretary was now required to certify that he had himself reached a "determin[ation]" that the released detainee would not likely engage in terrorist activity if repatriated or resettled. That change in the certification language was all-important.

When President Obama appointed a new State Department Special Envoy, Cliff Sloan, to speed the process of resettlement, we sought a meeting with him and in fact had such a meeting on September 9, 2013. Ambassador Sloan was cordial but gave no hint whether he would take any action to liberate Adel from Guantanamo. Although we communicated thereafter with Ambassador Sloan and a member of his staff, there were no outward signs of progress.

As time passed with no definite prospect for Adel's resettlement on the horizon, we decided that we had to stir the pot and did so by filing in January 2014 a Motion for Order of Release. We argued that Adel's indefinite detention after he had been cleared—at least twice—to leave Guantanamo violated his due process rights and that the Court had equitable power to order his release. In May 2014 Chief Judge Lamberth denied the motion on the "control[ling]" authority of his earlier decision in *Ahjam v. Obama*, in which the Court had held that a detainee had no standing to challenge the restrictions on transfers in the 2013 National Defense Authorization Act as an unconstitutional interference by Congress with the President's conduct of foreign affairs. Since our motion did not pose a standing issue, I found Chief Judge Lamberth's reliance on his earlier *Ahjam* decision inexplicable, but our motion was denied nevertheless.

Resettlement

Our hope kindled by the change in legislative language described above was reinforced when we learned that a delegation of officials had been sent by Uruguay to meet with U.S. officials and that six detainees—four Syrians, a Palestinian, and Adel—had been selected by Uruguay for resettlement. The Uruguayan delegation generously agreed to meet with U.S. counsel for the six and did so in February 2014, after which the delegation traveled to Guantanamo. They told the detainees that they would be required to learn Spanish, which posed no problem for Adel, who was fluent in Italian after having lived in that country for eight years.

On February 24, 2014, I received call from a member of Ambassador Sloan's office informing me that the Uruguayan government had offered Adel resettlement and that he had accepted the offer. Why would Uruguay, a small South American country with few Muslims, be willing to assume the burden of providing housing and otherwise integrating six previously detained Arabs into its society? The answer lay in the fact that the country's president, Jorge Mujica, had been imprisoned as a rebel leader for fourteen years by the previous totalitarian regime. He could envision himself in the detainees' position as could few other world leaders.

Uruguay had previously accepted some 300 Syrian refugees for resettlement and had a sizable population of individuals who had been born in other countries. When our government asked Uruguay to undertake that the resettled Guantanamo detainees would not leave the country for two years, President Mujica flatly refused, saying that once the detainees landed on Uruguayan soil, they would be "free men."

President Mujica came to Washington in May 2014 and met with President Obama. He may have had other purposes as well, but I am confident that he reiterated his country's willingness to accept six detainees. Still Secretary of Defense Hagel failed to submit the required certification to Congress until sometime in July. It has been reported in the press that a U.S. military transport was on the runway at Guantanamo on August 6 ready to transport the six detainees to Uruguay, but at that point the Uruguayan government balked because the transfer would occur too close to the presidential election scheduled to be held in October, and it was feared that the rightist party would use the arrival of the detainees as a diversion from the real issues in the election. Fortunately, President Mujica's party won the initial election as well as the runoff compelled by the relatively narrow margin in the initial election.

On Saturday evening, December 5, 2014, Adel and the other five detainees accepted by Uruguay were placed on a plane at Guantanamo and flown to Montevideo. Within days after their arrival, they were granted refugee status. We began making arrangements to travel to Uruguay, where we hoped to work with the Uruguayan government on the terms of Adel's resettlement, including accommodations, financial support, Spanish language training, and employment.

One month later, my colleague Anil Vasanji and I flew to Miami and thence to Montevideo, where we met up with another colleague, Jessica Klein, and her family entourage: her husband, mother, and two sons aged, respectively, two-and-a-half years and three months. At the time Jessica was on maternity leave from the firm. We met with Adel and the other detainees at a house owned by the labor union to which all workers in the country belonged. The union had agreed to provide temporary housing and food for the six men, who had also begun Spanish lessons.

During our four days in Uruguay, Anil and I met with senior officials of the U.S. Embassy, who were cordial and seemed genuinely interested in the fate of the six detainees. Indeed, when I wrote to those officials on my return to New York thanking them for meeting with me and expressing the hope that they would monitor the difficult integration of the men into Uruguayan society, the Chargé d'Affaires immediately responded by e-mail that "[w]e will certainly raise with the Uruguayan authorities the concerns you identified."

Jessica, Anil, and I also met with the labor union's Director of International Relations, Fernando Gambera, who interrupted his vacation to meet with us and showed up for the meeting in shorts and a T-shirt. He explained that the current situation was temporary and that a new Legislature would convene in late February and authorize the funds necessary to provide permanent housing, which would come from a supply of foreclosed homes. SEDU, the largest NGO in the country, would assume responsibility for making travel arrangements for family members who wished to join the men in Uruguay, as Adel told us was his mother's wish.

Adel and the other five former detainees were disappointed and frustrated at the unanticipated delay in receiving permanent housing and financial support. They had been deprived of the simple amenities of life for so long that they understandably had a sense of entitlement now that they were on free soil. They believed that former detainees resettled in other countries were living in better conditions, which I understand from other sources is not the case. I counseled patience and told Adel that he had arrived at an unfortunate time: virtually everyone was on summer holiday (I was not able to meet with any Uruguayan officials); Christmas had just passed; and the Legislature was not in session.

On Saturday, January 10, the day of my departure, we had a farewell picnic: Adel, Jessica and her family, Anil, Ibraham Qatabi (our friendly and indispensable Arab-English translator), and I. Adel cradled Jessica's infant son, Jonah, in his arms.

Then Adel, Ibraham, Mike Healey (Jessica's husband), and Anil, with occasional participation by Jessica's older son, Isaac, kicked around a soccer ball. I told Adel that with his resettlement, my lawyer-client relationship with him had ended, but that I hoped the friendship we had developed over the years would endure and that he would prosper in his new home country. There was a lump in my throat, and I think there was in Adel's also, when the time came for me to leave for the airport.

Adel El-Ouerghi lost twelve years of his life to Guantanamo and lost his wife as well. His first months in Uruguay were marked by disappointment and misunderstanding. He came to the country with high expectations—immediate private housing, eventual suitable employment, and the swift arrival of his mother from Tunisia—that were not met. The men were asked to work in the construction industry,

Adel El-Ouerghi holding Jonah Healey

but refused because they felt they were not physically or emotionally fit for manual labor. Adel became so frustrated that he told me he was thinking of protesting publicly on the grounds of the U.S. Embassy. I advised him not to do so.

On April 23, 2015, Adel and two other former detainees translated that thought into action, commencing a "sit-in" protest on the grounds of the U.S. Embassy. Both the U.S. and Uruguayan governments showed great restraint in permitting the protest, which received considerable publicity, to continue. It lasted for four weeks, ending on May 19 with a reported agreement, as to which there was almost immediate disagreement over its terms.

Ten days later the *Al Aribya* news service reported to my amazement that Adel and one other former detainee planned to marry, and on June 5 the Associated Press reported that Adel had that day married Roma Blanco, a twenty-four-year-old Uruguayan woman, who had a five-year-old son and who had converted to Islam four months earlier, taking the name Samira and renaming her son Mohammed. Samira had met Adel at a mosque. Their photograph was taken at the window of Adel's new apartment. I do not think I have ever seen a happier expression than Adel's in that photograph.

Adel had told me for years that he hoped to remarry and have a family, and I believe that goal in life had helped to keep him sane. It appeared that his dream may have been realized. On June 16, Jessica, Anil, and I talked with Adel and Samira to give them our warmest wishes for a long and happy married life. Adel's voice was brimming with enthusiasm.

I wish the story had ended at this point, but regrettably it has not. I read a news report a few months ago that Adel had been abusive to Samira and she had obtained a restraining order against him. The report further stated that Samira wished a divorce. This news was heartbreaking, but on reflection it should not have come as a surprise. Adel is still adjusting to life as a free man after more than twelve years in captivity. He is clearly struggling to adapt to his new freedom and to a strange land and different culture. I hope that he receives counseling and finds a job that will relieve him from being a ward of the state. His dream is to open a Tunisian restaurant. Whether or not he realizes that dream, I hope he finds peace.

* * *

When I undertook to represent Adel El-Ouerghi in the spring of 2005, many of my lawyer friends and colleagues applauded my having done so. But I was surprised and disappointed by the disapproving, if muted, reaction of others, who seemed to think that if Adel was confined at Guantanamo, he must have engaged in or actively supported terrorism. And, to their way of thinking, if he was a terrorist, he did not deserve counsel, certainly not counsel affiliated with a prestigious law firm. Perhaps I should not have been surprised by that reflexive condemnation, but I was surprised, and saddened as well. In fairness, I must quickly add that no one at my firm questioned, much less discouraged, the devotion by Jessica Klein, Anil Vassanji, and others of thousands of hours collectively to our representation of Adel El-Ouerghi.

My almost ten-year journey representing Adel was indescribably rewarding. I may not have persuaded a court to grant him habeas corpus. But I like to think that the knowledge that someone was fighting for him outside the walls of Guantanamo helped to sustain him through his ordeal.

I was reminded by my friend and fellow detainee counsel Mike Mone of the entry that John Adams—President, statesman, and one of our founding fathers—made in his diary, recalling late in life his representation of a British officer and British soldiers charged with murder after the Boston Massacre of 1770, in which five civilians died. Adams, who had been a young lawyer at the time, reflected that though he was torn by "anxiety" and subjected to "obloquy," that representation had been "one of the best pieces of service I ever rendered my country." Though I cannot and do not compare myself to John Adams, I feel about my representation of Adel El-Ouerghi as he did about his representation of the British officer and soldiers.

A CLOSING NOTE

I have been blessed with good fortune throughout my professional life:

– to have been interviewed by John Dooling, who personified the best of Sullivan & Cromwell and the legal profession;

– to have been asked by Judge Peck to take on significant pretrial and trial responsibilities in the Hudson & Manhattan condemnation case;

– to have played a lead role in other varied, unusual, and fascinating cases in the state and federal courts of New York, Pennsylvania, Ohio, Florida, Texas, Colorado, California, and Washington, D.C.;

– to have risen through the ranks to lead the New York City Bar Association and the American College of Trial Lawyers; and

– to have found ways to help both directly and indirectly individuals who could not obtain counsel: the poor, the otherwise disadvantaged, and even the outcast: a Guantanamo detainee.

Through the years (or, more accurately, decades), I have had wonderful colleagues at Sullivan & Cromwell to work with on my cases and the support of the firm in my "outside" activities.

Finally, I would not have had the strength to undertake all that I have done without the enduring support of my family.

All in all, it has been a long but very stimulating and very fulfilling journey.

Michael A. Cooper
March 2016

INDEX